THE RULE
OF
SAINT
BENEDICT

GW00808866

THE RULE
OF
SAINT
BENEDICT

TRANSLATED BY
PLACID MURRAY OSB

....

GLENSTAL ABBEY, IRELAND

2012

Published by Glenstal Abbey
Murroe, Co. Limerick, Ireland
www.glenstal.org

Copyright © Trustees of Glenstal Abbey 2012

ISBN 978-0-9572804-0-3

Cover design by Emmaus O'Herlihy O.S.B.
Production by INTYPE Design & Print Ltd, Limerick, Ireland.

TABLE OF CONTENTS

Table of Contents

Table of Contents

Table of Contents

INTRODUCTION

Since the sixth century the *Rule of St Benedict* has provided a sure spiritual guide for countless numbers of monks, nuns and oblates. Composed in an age beset by violence and instability, it became one of the foundational texts of Western Society, guiding Christians in their efforts to create a civilization of love. In our own age the spiritual riches of the *Rule* inspire and sustain men and women of goodwill, crossing boundaries of gender, race, denomination and calling while still remaining the bedrock of those whose primary vocation is to the cloister.

What, then, are St Benedict's guiding spiritual principles? What underpins for his followers the whole structure of Divine Office, work, administration, hospitality, reading, stability in the monastery, mutual forgiveness, obedience to the abbot and to one another, humility, perseverance together until death?

Let St Benedict himself give the answer in his final chapter:

> **Whoever you are therefore who are *hastening to the home country of heaven*, carry out this very small beginners' Rule, with Christ to help you; and then, under God's protection, you will arrive at those greater peaks of doctrine and of virtues which we have spoken above. Amen.**

Although now adapted to the needs of a wide variety of vocations, The *Rule of St. Benedict* was composed to meet the needs of a single monastic community of manageable size, which has to provide its own officers from within its own limited ranks. There was no pool of experts or trained men elsewhere—no 'Order' or 'Province'—that it could draw on. Moreover the vow of stability meant that the personnel of a monastery was not interchangeable with that of any other house. Life together lived together in prayer, work, reading and stability should shape and mature the individual characters in various directions. Through the lifelong daily testing of community life there would emerge an abbot, a cellarer, a guestmaster, a chanter, a doorkeeper, a novice master. The community needs all these other officials as well as an abbot. St Benedict has an eye out for them and on what kind of person each should be. Their jobs are not to be looked on as rungs in the ladder of promotion—each is a task complete and rounded off in itself which is every bit as necessary to the smooth running of the house as the abbot's.

St Benedict combines a minute organization of daily life, for instance of the daily round of the Divine Office, together with a latitude for eventual adaptations or for other solutions which might supersede his own. In former generations the problem of 'letter' and 'spirit' of the *Rule* hinged on 'observance'. Nowadays it turns on community prayer. The problem is far from being solved: how to remain faithful to St Benedict's spirit about the quantity and quality of community prayer, while changing the arrangements which he laid down.

St Benedict's disciplinary chapters—especially those legislating for 'excommunication'—cause embarrassment nowadays in some quarters. Nevertheless, one of the pearls of the *Rule* is contained in this section: chapter 27, 'What the abbot's care for the excommunicated should be.' We could not afford to forgo this most evangelical guidance.

About twenty chapters in the middle range of the *Rule* deal with administration. The very humane chapter 31, 'Of the monastery's Cellarer, what type of person he should be' sets the tone:

Things to be given out and things to be asked for shall be given out and asked for at appropriate times, so that in the house of God nobody be disturbed or distressed.

The present translation—now slightly revised—was first prepared for the English language edition of Abbot George Holzherr's *The Rule of Benedict, A Guide to Christian Living* (Four Courts Press, Dublin, 1994). St Benedict's scriptural quotations are italicized with the corresponding biblical references given in the appendix, 'The *Rule* and the Bible'. The traditional dates for reading the *Rule* three times a year are also provided.

I am grateful to P. Matthäus Rothenhäusler who first taught me to read the *Rule* for its own sake; to Jack Dwyer and Jimmy Backes for their assistance in preparing the text; and to my confrères, Senan Furlong, Colmán Ó Clabaigh, Martin Browne and Emmaus O'Herlihy for their efforts. Its publication constitutes a small act of thanksgiving for the grace of priestly ordination received seventy years ago at Subiaco.

Ut in omnibus glorificetur Deus

Placid Murray OSB

Glenstal Abbey

20 DECEMBER 2011

PROLOGUE

1 JANUARY | ¹Hear and heed, my son, the master's
2 MAY | teaching and bow the ear of your heart.
1 SEPTEMBER | Willingly take to yourself the loving
father's advice and fulfil it in what you do. ²Thus,
by laborious obedience will you return to him, from
whom you have withdrawn by idle disobedience.
³To you my word is now directed, whoever you are,
if you renounce self-will and grasp the tough, shin-
ing weapons of obedience, in order to serve the true
King, Christ, the Lord. ⁴First of all, with insistent
prayer, beg that he would bring to completion every
good that you set out to do. ⁵Now that he has num-

1

bered us with loving-kindness among his sons, he should never have to grieve over our bad lives. 6Rather we must obey him always with his gifts which he has implanted in us, so that, as an angered father, he will not some day disinherit his sons; 7still less, as a severe lord, grown angry by our misdeeds, deliver us as good-for-nothing servants to eternal punishment, because we did not wish to follow him to glory.

2 JANUARY | 8Let us then at long last get up because
3 MAY | scripture is calling us up with the words:
2 SEPTEMBER | *The hour has come to rise from sleep.* 9Let us open our eyes to the divinizing light, and with startled ears let us listen to what the divine voice is calling out every day, urging us: 10 *Today, if you should hear his voice, harden not your hearts.* 11And furthermore: *He who has ears to hear, let him hear what the Spirit is saying to the churches.* 12And what is he saying? *Come, O sons, listen to me; I will teach you the fear of the Lord.* 13 *Run while you have the light* of life, *so that the darkness* of death *may not overtake you.*

3 JANUARY | 14The Lord proclaims this to the con-
4 MAY | course of people, where he is looking for
3 SEPTEMBER | his workman, and he continues further:
15 *Who is the man, who loves life, and wants to see good days?* 16If you hear this and answer 'I', then God says

to you: 17If you wish to have true and eternal life,
then *keep your tongue from evil and your lips from
uttering lies; turn from evil and do good, seek peace and
pursue it.* 18If you do this, my *eyes shall rest upon* you,
and my *ears shall hear* your *prayers,* and *before you
call to me, I shall say: here I am.* 19What sound could
be sweeter, beloved brothers, than this voice of the
Lord, who is inviting us? 20See, in his loving-
kindness the Lord points out to us the path to life.

4 JANUARY | 21Let us gird ourselves then with faith,
5 MAY | let us fulfil our duty with all fidelity
4 SEPTEMBER | and, under the guidance of the Gospel
let us step forward on the ways of the Lord, so that
we may be given to see him, who has called us into
his kingdom. 22If we wish to live in the tent of his
kingdom, we must hasten ahead with good deeds;
otherwise we shall never get there. 23But let us
question the Lord with the Prophet: *Lord, who shall
be a guest in your tent? Who may linger on your holy
hill?* 24Let us hear, brothers, what the Lord answers
to this question, as he points out to us the way to his
tent. 25He says: *the man of blameless life, who does
what is right;* 26*who speaks the truth from his heart
and does not slander with his tongue;* 27 *who never
wrongs a friend and tells no tales against his neighbour,*
28who expels from the field of vision of his heart the

evil one, the devil, who is whispering something to him, together with his suggestions, and brings him to nothing; who grasps such devil's brood of thoughts and shatters them on Christ; 29who fears the Lord and does not boast of his faithful service, but rather believes that everything good that is peculiarly his own, exceeds his own possibility and is the Lord's work; 30such men glorify the Lord, who is at work in them, and they say with the prophet: *Not to us, Lord, not to us, but to your name give the glory.* 31Thus even the Apostle Paul in his teaching did not ascribe anything to himself; he says: *by the grace of God I am, what I am.* 32And once again he says: *If a man must boast, let him boast of the Lord.*

5 JANUARY | 33That is why the Lord says in the
6 MAY | Gospel: *He who hears these words of*
5 SEPTEMBER | *mine and acts on them, I shall compare him to a wise man, who built his house on rock.* 34*The floods came, the winds blew and beat upon that house, but it did not fall; it was founded upon rock.* 35With these words the Lord concludes his discourse. Now, day by day, he is waiting for us to respond with deeds to these holy urgings of his. 36That is why the days of this life are prolonged for us as a reprieve to reform our evil ways— 37the Apostle says so: *Do you not know that God's patience is urging you to repent?*

38For in his goodness the Lord says: *I desire not the death of the wicked man, but that he return and live.*

6 JANUARY
7 MAY
6 SEPTEMBER

39Brothers, we have now asked the Lord, who may live in his tent, and we have learned what is demanded of a dweller; if only we fulfil the duties of one who is to live in it. 40We must therefore get heart and body ready for service under holy obedience to these orders. 41But because our nature does not have enough strength for this, let us ask the Lord to send us the help of his grace. 42If we wish to escape punishment in the realm of death, and attain to everlasting life, we must, at present—43while our time lasts, as long as we are in this body, and can still fulfil all this in the light of this life—44hasten with rapid steps and do what will help us for eternity.

7 JANUARY
8 MAY
7 SEPTEMBER

45We intend therefore to found a school for the Lord's service. 46In its structures, we hope to arrange nothing harsh, nothing oppressive. 47But if for some good reason the requirements exacted be a trifle austere in order to rectify faults and safeguard love, 48you should not, disconcerted by sudden fright, shrink back from the way of salvation, which cannot but be narrow at its opening. 49But as for him who is who is making progress in the religious life and in faith, his heart opens wide, and with the joy that is too great for words and which comes from love, he runs ahead in the way of God's commandments. 50So let us never let go of his instructions, but rather hold fast to his teaching in the monastery until death and share in patience in Christ's sufferings so that we may also merit to have a share in his kingdom. Amen.

1

OF THE TYPES OF MONKS

8 JANUARY | [1]It is clear that there are four types of
9 MAY | monk. [2]The first is that of the cenobites,
8 SEPTEMBER | who serve under rule and abbot in the
monastery. [3]The second type are the anchorites or her-
mits. After a long testing-time in the monastery—not
in the first fervour of a monk's life—[4]they learned to
fight against the devil through the skill acquired from
the support of many. [5]They were well trained in the
ranks of the brothers for the single-handed combat of
the desert. Fearless and even without another's encour-
agement they are able now, with God's help, to fight
against vices of flesh and thoughts, unaided and alone.

9 JANUARY | [6]A third, quite dreadful type of monk
10 MAY | are the sarabaites. Never tested by a rule,
9 SEPTEMBER | never taught by experience, they have
never become like gold from the furnace; instead they
are in nature soft as lead. [7]In their occupations they
still keep faith with the world and openly lie to God
by their tonsure. [8]In twos or threes or even singly they
live without a shepherd, withdrawn within their own,
not the Lord's, sheepfolds. What their appetites desire
is for them the law. [9]All their own views and wishes

7

they call holy; what they do not want they consider not to be allowed. [10]The fourth type of monk are those called gyrovagues. Their whole life long they flit from country to country, staying as guests for three or four days in the cells of various monks; [11]always adrift and never stable, slaves of their own whims and the pleasures of the palate, and in all points worse than the sarabaites. [12]Of the deplorable life of all these monks let us rather keep silence than speak. [13]Let us disregard them, and, with God's help, set about to give the strongest type, the cenobites.

2

WHAT THE ABBOT SHOULD BE LIKE

10 JANUARY
11 MAY
10 SEPTEMBER

[1]To be worthy to preside over the monastery, let the abbot always be aware of what he is called; let him make the name of 'superior' a reality by his deeds. [2]Faith believes that he deputizes in the monastery for Christ, since he is designated by a name proper to Christ, [3]as the Apostle says: *You have received the spirit of adoption of sons, whereby we cry: abba 'father'*. [4]Therefore the abbot has a duty not to teach, set up or order anything which deviates from the Lord's commandment, [5]rather what he orders and what he teaches should

penetrate the hearts of his disciples as a leaven of divine justice. 6Let the abbot constantly remember that at God's awe-inspiring judgement both matters will be under scrutiny: his teaching and the disciples' obedience. 7And let the abbot know that the responsibility falls on the shepherd when the householder discovers a loss of yield among his sheep. 8On the other hand it will be equally true: if the shepherd has bestowed all pastoral care on a restless and disobedient flock, and applied every healing skill to their diseased ways of acting, 9he will be acquitted at the Lord's judgement, and may say to the Lord with the prophet: *I have not hidden your justice within my heart; I have declared your truth and your salvation; but they have despised and disdained me.* 10And at last on the sheep, who in disobedience set themselves in opposition to his care, the punishment will come: triumphant death.

11 JANUARY | 11He therefore who assumes the name
12 MAY | of 'abbot' must lead his disciples with
11 SEPTEMBER | a twofold teaching; 12that is to say: let him show what is good and holy by deeds rather than by words. To teachable disciples let him expound the Lord's commands in words; to the hard-hearted, however, and the more simpleminded let his deeds demonstrate God's precepts. 13Whenever he has

taught his disciples that something is harmful, let him show by his deeds that one ought not do it. Otherwise he could be *preaching to others and himself be found rejected.* 14And will not God say to him some day on account of his sins: *What right have you to recite my statutes or take my covenant on your lips? For you hate discipline, and you cast my words behind you.* 15And *you saw the splinter in your brother's eye, and did not see the timber beam in your own.*

12 JANUARY | 16Let him show no favouritism within
13 MAY | the monastery. 17Let him not love one
12 SEPTEMBER | more than another, unless he finds one who is better at good actions and obedience. 18He who came from the status of freeman should not have precedence over the monk who came from the state of slavery, except on some other basis that is reasonable. 19If, on the basis of justice, the abbot decides to do so, he may also do the same for the rank of anyone at all. If this be not the case, let each keep his own place; 20for *whether slave or freeman, in Christ we are all one,* and under the same Lord bear the burden of the same duties of service; because *with God there is no respect of persons.* 21For one reason only are we preferred by him, if we prove to be better than others in good works, and remain humble. 22Let the abbot therefore show an equal

love of all, let the same standards be set for all, in line with what each one deserves.

13 JANUARY

14 MAY

13 SEPTEMBER | 23As a teacher, let the abbot always follow the example of the apostle who says: *reprove, entreat, rebuke.* 24That is to say: let him vary sternness with affability according to time and circumstance, showing now the severe face of a master, and again the loving heart of a father. 25The lawless and the restless therefore he should sharply reprove, the obedient, however, the meek, and the patient he should entreat to advance even still more. The careless and the disdainful he should rebuke and punish: such is our advice. 26He should not overlook the sins of the guilty, rather, immediately at the outset let him, as best he can, cut out these sins by the roots. Let him reflect that otherwise the same danger threatens him which befell Eli, the priest of Shiloh. 27Those of upright and intelligent cast of mind he should, at the first and second warning, caution in words; 28the shameless and the callous, the proud and the disobedient he should, at the first onset of sin, punish with the rod or with corporal punishment. Surely he knows that it is written: *Words will not correct a fool.* 29And again: *Beat your son with the stick and you will save his soul from death.*

14 JANUARY | 30Let the abbot constantly remember
15 MAY | what he is; remember the name he bears;
14 SEPTEMBER | and let him know that the man to whom
more is given, of him much more is required. 31Let
him realise, what a difficult and toilsome task he has
taken on: to be a leader of souls, a servant of many
characters: coaxing one, rebuking another, reasoning
with a third. 32Let him make himself congenial to all
and adapt himself to all according to each one's char-
acter and capacities, so that, in the flock committed
to him, he not only suffers no loss, but may rejoice
to see the good flock thrive.

15 JANUARY | 33Above all, he should not close his
16 MAY | eyes to, or underrate the salvation of
15 SEPTEMBER | souls entrusted to him by bestowing
more care on things that pass, things of this earth,
things that perish. 34Rather let him ever keep before
his mind that he has undertaken to lead souls for
whom he will one day also have to give account.
35And let him not make excuses because of what are
perhaps insufficient means; let him remember the
word of scripture: *Seek first the kingdom of God and
his justice, and all these things shall be given you besides.*
36And further: *Nothing is lacking to those who fear
him.* 37Let him know that he who undertakes to lead
souls, must prepare himself to render an account of

them. 38Let him be quite certain that, on the day of judgement, he will have to give an account to the Lord, for as many souls as there are brothers under his care, and, beyond doubt, for his own soul too. 39And so, always fearful of the coming scrutiny which he will have to undergo as shepherd for the sheep committed to his care, he is rendered watchful about his own statement of accounts, while he goes guarantor for those of others. 40And while his words of advice help others to amend, he himself, in the process, sheds his own faults.

3

ON CONVENING THE BROTHERS FOR CONSULATION

16 JANUARY | 1Whenever there are matters of
17 MAY | importance in the monastery, let the
16 SEPTEMBER | abbot convene the whole community,
and himself state what is at issue. 2And listening to the advice of the brothers let him weigh it up in his own mind; and when he has decided what is the more useful course, let him follow it out. 3But the reason we have said that all should be convened for consultation is that the Lord often reveals the better thing to a younger person. 4Let the brothers

however, give their opinion with all the submission of humility, nor let them presume to defend their own point of view with insolence. 5Let the decision depend rather on the abbot, and let all obey what he will have judged to be the more salutary course. 6But just as it befits disciples to obey the master, so it is incumbent on him to make all arrangements with foresight and justice.

17 JANUARY | 7In all things therefore let all follow the
18 MAY | tutelage of the Rule, nor let anyone de-
17 SEPTEMBER | fiantly deviate from it. 8Let no one in
the monastery follow the pull of his own heart, 9nor let anyone presume to have words with his abbot in an insolent manner, or outside the monastery. 10If he have presumed this, let him undergo the discipline of the Rule. 11However, let the abbot himself do everything in the fear of God and with observance of the Rule, fully aware that he will have to render an account of all his decisions to God, the just judge. 12If, however, some less important matters of the monastery's affairs have to be attended to, let him consult the seniors only, according to the word of Scripture: 13*Do everything with consultation, and you will have no regrets when the deed is done.*

4

THE TOOLS OF GOOD WORKS: WHAT ARE THEY?

18 JANUARY | [1]First: *to love the Lord God from a full*
19 MAY | *heart, with the whole soul, with all one's*
18 SEPTEMBER | *strength.* [2]Then: *the neighbour as if oneself.* [3]Then: *not to kill.* [4]*Not to commit adultery.* [5]*Not to steal.* [6]*Not to sin by concupiscence.* [7]*Not to bear false witness.* [8]To respect everyone. [9]And *not to do to another what one does not wish done to oneself.* [10]*To deny one's very self to oneself,* in order to follow Christ. [11]*To discipline the body.* [12]Not to be enamoured of soft living. [13]To love fasting. [14]To give new heart to the poor. [15]*To clothe a naked person.* [16]*To visit a sick person.* [17]To bury a dead person. [18]To be a support in time of trouble. [19]To comfort one who is saddened.

19 JANUARY | [20]To make oneself an outsider to the
20 MAY | ways of the world. [21]To put nothing
19 SEPTEMBER | above the love for Christ. [22]Not to bring anger to a head. [23]Not to keep a time for an outburst of temper. [24]Not to retain deceit in one's heart. [25]Not to offer an insincere peace. [26]Not to be unfaithful to love. [27]*Not to swear, lest one swear falsely.* [28]*To utter the truth from heart and mouth.* [29]*Not to*

15

repay wrong with wrong. 30To do no wrong, but in fact to suffer patiently wrongs done to oneself. 31 *To love one's enemies.* 32 *Not to return insult for insult, to return rather a blessing.* 33 *To suffer persecution for justice's sake.* 34Not to be *arrogant.* 35 *Not a heavy drinker.* 36Not immoderate in eating. 37Not drowsy; 38not *lazy,* 39not given to criticizing. 40Not a detractor. 41To entrust one's hope to God. 42On seeing something good in oneself, to refer it to God, not to self, 43realizing, however, always that evil was one's own doing, and to impute it to oneself.

20 JANUARY

21 MAY

20 SEPTEMBER 44To fear Judgement Day. 45To be terrified of hell. 46To yearn for eternal life with all spiritual longing. 47To look death daily in the eye. 48At every moment to keep guard over the actions of one's life. 49To know for certain everywhere that God is looking at one. 50When bad thoughts slip into one's heart to dash them immediately against Christ and to reveal them to a spiritual elder. 51To guard one's mouth from evil or depraved talk. 52Not to love much talking. 53Not to speak foolish or facetious words. 54Not to love much or loud laughter. 55To listen with pleasure to the holy readings. 56To prostrate oneself frequently in prayer. 57With tears and sighing daily to confess your past sins to God in prayer. 58For the future to

rectify these same faults. *59Not to gratify the cravings of the flesh.* 60To hate self-will. 61To obey the abbot's commands in everything, even were he himself— which God forbid—to act differently; remembering that command of the Lord: *Do what they tell you, but not what they do.* 62Not to want to be called a saint, before you are one; first be so, that you may be more genuinely called so.

21 JANUARY | 63Day by day to fulfil by deeds what

22 MAY | God commands. 64To love purity.

21 SEPTEMBER | 65To hate nobody. 66Not to entertain jealousy. 67Not to indulge in rivalry. 68To have no craving for controversy. 69To shun pride. 70And to respect the elderly. 71To love the younger. 72Out of love for Christ to pray for one's enemies. 73To make peace with an opponent before sunset. 74And to never despair God's mercy. 75See, these are the tools of the art of the Spirit. 76When day and night they will have been acted on by us without respite, and accounted for on the Day of Judgement, that reward will be paid out to us by the Lord which he himself has promised: *77Eye has not seen nor ear heard what things God has prepared for those who love him.* 78The monastery enclosure and stability in the community constitute, however, the workshop where we labour diligently at all these things.

5

OF OBEDIENCE

22 JANUARY
23 MAY
22 SEPTEMBER [1]The first step in humility is to obey without delay. [2]This is appropriate for those who value nothing dearer to themselves than Christ. [3-4]As soon as anything has been ordered by a superior, just as if it were God's command, they cannot brook a delay in carrying it out—because of the holy service they have professed, or for the fear of hell, and the glory of eternal life. [5]The Lord says of these: *At the ear's hearing he obeyed me.* [6]And, besides, to teachers he says: *He who hears you, hears me.* [7]Therefore, such as these immediately leaving aside what is their own, and forsaking self-will, [8]leaving unfinished the work they were at, with hands at the ready, and the step of obedience close by, they follow directly with deeds the voice of him who commands. [9]And as it were in one second, both things, the previously mentioned order of the master and the completed task of the disciple, are quickly finished together, in the speed of the fear of God. [10]There presses on them the love of advancing towards eternal life; [11]therefore, they seize the narrow way, about which

the Lord says: *Narrow is the way that leads to life,*
12so that, resident in community monasteries, not
living by their own free will, nor obeying their own
desires and pleasures, but walking by the judgement
and orders of another, they desire to have an abbot
rule them. 13There is no doubt that such as these
imitate that maxim of the Lord in which he says:
*I have come not to do my own will but the will of
him who sent me.*

23 JANUARY | 14But this obedience itself will then
24 MAY | be pleasing to God and delightful to
23 SEPTEMBER | men, if what is commanded be done
not with fear, nor with delay, nor half-heartedly,
nor with grumbling nor with an unwilling answer,
15because obedience shown to superiors is given to
God. He in fact has said: *He who hears you, hears
me.* 16And it ought to be given by the disciple with
good humour, because *God loves a cheerful giver.*
17For if a disciple obeys with ill grace and com-
plains, not only by word of mouth, but even in
his heart, 18though he should fulfil the command,
nevertheless it will no longer be accepted by God,
who is looking at his discontented heart. 19And for
such a deed he will obtain no grace. Rather, he will
incur the punishment due to murmurers if he does
not amend with satisfaction.

6

OF RESERVE IN SPEECH

¹Let us do what the prophet is saying: I said: *I will guard my ways so as not to sin by my tongue. I put a guard at my mouth, I fell silent and was humbled and did not speak of good things.* ²Here the prophet is showing that if at times for reticence's sake one must refrain from conversation that is good, how much more, because of punishment for sin, ought one to cease from words that are bad. ³Therefore, because of the serious nature of reticence, let permission to talk be rarely granted to perfect disciples, even for good, holy, and edifying conversations; ⁴for it is written: *In much speaking you will not escape sin.* ⁵And in another passage: *Death and life are in the hands of the tongue.* ⁶To speak and to teach, indeed, befits the master; to be silent and to listen becomes the disciple. ⁷Therefore, if requests are to be made of a superior, let them be asked for with all humility and respectful submission. ⁸Ribaldry, however, and idle words provoking laughter we condemn everywhere with a perpetual ban, nor do we allow a disciple to open his mouth for such talk.

7

OF HUMILITY

25 JANUARY | ¹Sacred Scripture cries out to us,
26 MAY | brothers. It is saying: *Everyone who*
25 SEPTEMBER | *makes himself great will be humbled, and*
he who humbles himself will be made great. ²In saying
this therefore, it shows us that all aggrandizement is
of the nature of pride. ³The prophet declares that he
avoids this. He says: *Lord my heart is not lifted up, my*
eyes are not haughty, nor have I walked in great things,
nor in marvels above me. ⁴But what will happen *if I*
did not feel humbly if I exalted my soul? Like a weaned
child on its mother so you will punish my soul.

26 JANUARY | ⁵Now, brothers, if we wish to reach
27 MAY | the summit of highest humility and
26 SEPTEMBER | if we want to arrive with speed at that
heavenly exaltation to which one climbs by the
humility of the present life, ⁶that ladder must be
raised up by our mounting actions; that ladder
which appeared to Jacob in the dream and on which
were shown to him angels coming down and going
up. ⁷There can be no doubt that that descent and
ascent is to be understood by us as nothing else but

21

to come down by aggrandizement, to go up by humility. 8The ladder itself indeed raised up is our life in the world, which is raised up to heaven by the Lord, when the heart has been humbled. 9We say that our body and soul are the sides of this ladder: into these sides the divine call has inserted various rungs to be climbed of humility and discipline.

27 JANUARY 10The first rung of humility then is
28 MAY if he absolutely avoids forgetfulness,
27 SEPTEMBER 11always putting the fear of God before his eyes, always remembering everything that God commanded, always turning over in his mind that hell burns up for their sins those who despise God, and that eternal life is prepared for those who fear God. 12And keeping himself at every moment from sins and vices, that is of thought, tongue, hands, feet, and self-will, and the desires of the flesh too, 13let a man consider that he is watched from heaven by God at every moment, and that in every place his deeds are seen by the eye of the godhead and are reported at every instant by angels. 14The prophet points this out to us when he shows that God is ever present in our thoughts. He says: *God is scrutinizing heart and loins;* 15and again: *The Lord is aware of men's thoughts;* 16and again he says: *You understood my thoughts from afar* 17and: *Because man's thought*

will make confession to you. ¹⁸On the other hand, in order to be on the alert about his bad thoughts, let the useful brother always keep saying in his heart: *Then shall I be sinless before him if I shall have kept myself from my iniquity.*

28 JANUARY | ¹⁹We are accordingly forbidden to do
29 MAY | our own will since Scripture says to us:
28 SEPTEMBER | *And turn away from the acts of your will.*
²⁰And similarly we ask the Lord in the Prayer that his will be done in us. ²¹We are rightly therefore taught not to do our own will, when we avoid what Sacred Scripture says: *There are ways which are thought by men to be straight, whose end swallows up in deepest hell.* ²²And when again we dread what has been said of the negligent: *They have become corrupt and abominable in their wills.* ²³And in the desires of the flesh let us believe that God is always present to us in such a way as the prophet says: *All my desire is before you.* ²⁴Evil desire must therefore be avoided because death is lurking at the threshold of delight. ²⁵This is why Scripture commanded: *Do not follow your lusts.*

29 JANUARY | ²⁶Therefore *if the eyes of the Lord are*
30 MAY | *keeping watch over the good and the bad*
29 SEPTEMBER | ²⁷and *the Lord is ever looking down from heaven on the children of men, to see if there be one who*

23

is wise and seeks God, 28and if the works we do are reported to the Lord daily, day and night, by the angels assigned to us, 29then, brothers, as the prophet says in the psalm, we must take care at every moment, lest God see us at any moment turned aside to evil and become useless 30and sparing us at present, because he is loving and waits for us to change for the better, he says to us in the future: *These things you have done, and I kept silence.*

30 JANUARY | 31To be on the second rung of humility
31 MAY | is not to be in love with self-will, not to
30 SEPTEMBER | be delighted at fulfilling one's desires;
32but to imitate in practice that what the Lord says: *I have not come to do my will but his will who sent me.* 33Scripture also says: "Self-will gets punished, compulsion engenders a crown."

31 JANUARY | 34To be on the third rung of humility is
1 JUNE | out of love for God to submit oneself to
1 OCTOBER | a superior in total obedience, imitating
the Lord, of whom the Apostle says: made *obedient unto death.*

1 FEBRUARY | 35To be on the fourth rung of humility
2 JUNE | is to embrace patience, silently and
2 OCTOBER | consciously, if in the obedience itself difficult and contrary things, or even insults of

whatever kind are brought on, ³⁶and to bear up, not to grow weary or leave; Scripture has said: *whoever holds out to the end will be saved.* ³⁷Again: *Let your heart be strong and wait for the Lord.* ³⁸And showing that the faithful one ought to put up with everything, no matter how contrary, for the Lord, it says in the person of those who suffer: *For your sake we are being slain all day long; we are looked upon as sheep to be slaughtered.* ³⁹And certain of the hope of divine reward they go on with joy to say: *Yet in all this we are more than conquerors because of him who loved us.* ⁴⁰And again in another passage of Scripture: *You have tested us, God, you have refined us like silver; you let us fall into the net, you laid heavy burdens on our back.* ⁴¹And to show that we ought to be under a superior, it goes on to say: *You placed men over our heads.* ⁴²But fulfilling the Lord's precept by patience in adversities and insults *struck on one cheek they offer also the other, to him who takes tunic they let him have cloak as well, requisitioned to go one mile they go two.* ⁴³In company with the Apostle Paul *they put up with false brothers* and *endure persecution,* and *bless those who curse* them.

2 FEBRUARY
3 JUNE
3 OCTOBER | ⁴⁴To be on the fifth rung of humility is through a humble confession not to conceal from one's abbot all the bad thoughts that come to one's heart nor the bad things

one has secretly done. 45Scripture urges us in this matter: *Lay bare your way to the Lord and hope in him.* 46And again it says: *Confess to the Lord for he is good, for his mercy is for ever.* 47And the prophet once more: *I acknowledged my sin to you, my guilt I covered not.* 48*I said: accusing myself, I will confess my offences to the Lord, and you forgave the guilt of my heart.*

3 FEBRUARY
4 JUNE
4 OCTOBER

49To be on the sixth rung of humility is for a monk to be content with all that is cheapest and most marginal, and in all that is enjoined on him, to judge himself to be a bad workman, an unworthy one, 50saying to himself with the prophet: *I was brought down to nothing and knew it not; I was like a brute beast in your presence; yet with you I shall always be.*

4 FEBRUARY
5 JUNE
5 OCTOBER

51To be on the seventh rung of humility is not merely to declare with one's tongue that one is lower and of less account than all, but even to believe it in one's heart of hearts, 52humbling oneself and saying with the prophet: *But as for me, I am a worm and no man, the scorn of men and despised by the people.* 53*I have been exalted and humbled and confounded.* 54And again: *It has done me good that you humbled me and I may learn your commandments.*

5 FEBRUARY | ⁵⁵To be on the eighth rung of humility
6 JUNE | is for a monk to do nothing except what
6 OCTOBER | is encouraged by the common rule of
the monastery and the example of the superiors.

6 FEBRUARY | ⁵⁶To be on the ninth rung of humility
7 JUNE | is for a monk to forbid his tongue to
7 OCTOBER | speak, and, maintaining reserve, not to
speak until questioned. ⁵⁷Scripture shows that *where
words are many, sin is not wanting.* And: ⁵⁸*The talk-
ative man does not find footing in the land.*

7 FEBRUARY | ⁵⁹To be on the tenth rung of humility
8 JUNE | is to be not inconsiderately quick to
8 OCTOBER | laugh; because it is written: *The fool
raises his voice in laughter.*

8 FEBRUARY | ⁶⁰To be on the eleventh rung of
9 JUNE | humility is for a monk, when talking,
9 OCTOBER | to speak gently and without laughing,
humbly and with seriousness, with good sense, in few
words, and not in a noisy voice, ⁶¹as it is written: "A
man is recognized as wise when his words are few."

9 FEBRUARY | ⁶²To be on the twelfth rung of humility
10 JUNE | is for a monk to reveal to all who see
10 OCTOBER | him humility not only of heart, but of
his very body. ⁶³That is, with head ever bowed and

27

looks fixed on the ground, at the Work of God,
in the oratory, in the monastery, in the garden, on
the road, in the field, wherever he is sitting, walking
or standing, 64at every moment let him consider
himself guilty on account of his sins, and already
made present to the fearful Judgement, 65saying
always in his heart what that tax-gatherer in the
Gospel said with his eyes fixed on the ground:
*Lord, I am not worthy, I a sinner, to raise my eyes to
the heavens.* 66And again with the prophet: *I am
stooped and bowed down profoundly.* 67Therefore,
when he has climbed all these rungs of humility,
a monk will immediately come to that *love of God
which* when *perfect casts out fear.* 68By this love,
without any trouble, as it were naturally, by habit,
he will begin to keep everything which hitherto
he used to observe not without fear, 69no longer
now by the fear of hell but by the love of Christ,
and the good habit itself, and the delight of virtues.
70By the Holy Spirit the Lord will deign to demon-
strate these things in his workman, clean from vices
and sins.

8

OF THE DIVINE OFFICES IN THE NIGHTS

10 FEBRUARY | [1]In winter time, that is from the first
11 JUNE | of November until Easter, taking every-
11 OCTOBER | thing into due consideration, they shall
get up at the eighth hour of the night, [2]so as to sleep
for a little more than half the night, and rise when
digestion is completed. [3]The brothers who need to
do so shall employ the time over after Vigils in going
over the Psalter or the readings. [4]From Easter however until November as mentioned let the timing be
such that the brothers may go out for the necessities
of nature during a very brief interval after Vigils.
Lauds, which are to be celebrated at first light, shall
follow immediately.

9

HOW MANY PSALMS ARE TO BE SUNG
AT THE NIGHT HOURS

11 FEBRUARY | [1]In winter time, as defined above, begin
12 JUNE | with the versicle, to be said three times:
12 OCTOBER | *Lord, you will open my lips, and my mouth
shall declare your praise.* [2]To this shall be added Psalm 3,

29

and *Glory be.* 3After this, Psalm 94, with antiphon, or at least chanted. 4Then shall follow an Ambrosian hymn, then six psalms with antiphons. 5When these have been said, after the versicle, the abbot shall give a blessing. And all being seated on the stools three lessons shall be read by the brothers in turn from the book on the lectern; three responsories to be sung between these readings. 6Two responsories are to be said without *Glory be*, after the third reading however the chanter says the *Glory be.* 7When the chanter intones this, let all immediately rise from their seats for the honour and reverence due to the Holy Trinity. 8The books of divine authority, as well of the Old as of the New Testaments shall be read at Vigils, as also the commentaries on them which have been made by renowned and orthodox Catholic Fathers. 9After these three readings then, the remaining six psalms are to follow, to be sung with Alleluia. 10After these, there shall follow a reading from the Apostle, to be said by heart, and a versicle, and the supplication of the litany, that is *Kyrie eleison.* That is how Vigils end.

10

HOW THE NIGHT PRAISE IS TO BE CELEBRATED IN THE SUMMER

12 FEBRUARY | 1From Easter however until the first
13 JUNE | of November, let the full quantity of
13 OCTOBER | psalmody be maintained as said above:
2with the proviso that on account of the short nights the readings from the book are never read. Instead of these three readings one shall be said by heart from the Old Testament, to be followed by a short responsory. 3And all the rest shall be fulfilled as stipulated, that is, that not counting the third and ninety fourth psalms, never less than a quantity of twelve psalms shall be said at the night Vigils.

11

HOW VIGILS ARE TO BE CELEBRATED ON SUNDAYS

13 FEBRUARY | 1For Vigils on Sundays they shall rise
14 JUNE | earlier. 2In these Vigils the structure
14 OCTOBER | to be maintained is: six psalms and the
versicle having been sung, as we have arranged above, and all being seated on the benches in an orderly way,

by rank, four readings with their responsories shall be read from a book, as we said above. 3In this regard the *Glory be* is to be sung by the chanter only in the fourth responsory. When he intones it, all shall at once stand up, respectfully. 4After these readings there shall follow the other six psalms in numerical order, with antiphons like the preceding ones, and a versicle. 5After this, four lessons shall again be read, with their responsories, as arranged above. 6After these let there be said three canticles from the Prophets, as selected by the abbot; these canticles are sung with Alleluia. 7A versicle also shall be said, and after the blessing given by the abbot, four other readings are read from the New Testament, as arranged above. 8After the fourth responsory the abbot shall intone the hymn *Te Deum laudamus.* 9When this is said through, the abbot shall read the lesson from the Gospels, while all stand with respect and fear. 10When this has been read let all answer: *Amen*; and the abbot follows on immediately with the hymn *Te decet laus.* And after the blessing let them start Lauds. 11This order of Vigils is to be kept identical in all seasons, both of summer and winter, 12unless perhaps—which God forbid—they are late in getting up, and the readings or responsories have to be somewhat shortened. 13Every precaution however is to be taken that this do not occur; but if it should occur, let him through whose neglect it came about, do fitting satisfaction for it to God in the oratory.

12

HOW THE SOLEMN MORNING OFFICE IS TO BE CELEBRATED

14 FEBRUARY | ¹On Sundays at Morning Office Psalm
15 JUNE | 66 is to be said first, without antiphon,
15 OCTOBER | straight on. ²After this, say Psalm 50
with Alleluia. ³Then say 117 and 62. ⁴Then the
Benedicite and the psalms of praise, a reading from
the Apocalypse, by heart, Ambrosian hymn, versicle,
canticle from the Gospel book, litany, and so end.

13

HOW THE MORNING OFFICE IS TO BE SAID ON FERIAL DAYS

15 FEBRUARY | ¹On ferial days, however, the solemn
16 JUNE | Morning Office shall be celebrated as
16 OCTOBER | follows: ²Psalm 66 said without anti-
phon as on Sunday, at a slightly slower pace, so that
all may be in for Psalm 50, which is to be said with

antiphon. 3After this, two other psalms are said, according to custom, i.e. 4Monday, 5 and 35; 5Tuesday, 42 and 56; 6Wednesday, 63 and 64; 7Thursday, 87 and 89; 8Friday, 75 and 91; 9on Saturday however 142 and the Deuteronomy canticle divided in two by *Glory be* said twice. 10On the other days, however, a canticle is to be sung, each one to its own day, as the Roman Church sings them. 11After which there follow the psalms of praise, next a reading from the Apostle recited by heart, responsory, Ambrosian hymn, versicle, canticle from the Gospel book, litany, and so end.

16 FEBRUARY | 12Besides, the Morning and Evening
17 JUNE | Office should never come to a close
17 OCTOBER | without the Lord's Prayer being said in full at the end by the superior in the hearing of all, on account of the thorny scandals which have a habit of springing up, 13so that challenged by the promise of the very Prayer itself in which they say: *Forgive us as we forgive*, they may purge themselves of this kind of vice. 14At the other Offices, let the final part only of the prayer be said aloud, so that all may reply: *But deliver us from evil.*

14

HOW VIGILS ARE TO BE CELEBRATED ON BIRTHDAYS OF THE SAINTS

17 FEBRUARY | 1On the feasts of saints and on all
18 JUNE | solemnities do as we have said should
18 OCTOBER | be done on the Lord's Day, 2except that
psalms, antiphons, and readings appropriate to the
day be said. 3However, let the structure described
above be adhered to.

15

ALLELUIA: AT WHAT SEASONS IS IT TO BE SAID?

18 FEBRUARY | 1From holy Easter until Pentecost,
19 JUNE | alleluia shall be said without exception
19 OCTOBER | both in the psalms and in the responsor-
ies. 2From Pentecost, however, until the beginning of
Lent say it every night only with the last six psalms of
Nocturns. 3On every Sunday outside Lent sing with
Alleluia: canticles, Morning Prayer, first Hour, third
Hour, sixth Hour, ninth Hour; Evening Prayer, on the
other hand, with antiphon. 4Responsories are never to
be said with Alleluia, except from Easter to Pentecost.

16

HOW THE DIVINE OFFICES ARE TO BE CELEBRATED IN THE COURSE OF THE DAY

[1]As the prophet says: *Seven times a day I have given you praise.* [2]This sacred sevenfold number will be fulfilled by us, if in the morning, at the first Hour, at the third Hour, at the sixth Hour, at the ninth Hour, at evening and at Compline time, we acquit ourselves of the duties of our subject state, [3]because it was of these daytime Hours he said: *Seven times a day I have given you praise.* [4]For the very same prophet says of the night Vigils: *I rose at midnight to give you praise.* [5]Let us then at these times give praise to our Creator for the judgements of his justice, that is, at Lauds, Prime, Terce, Sext, None, Vespers and Compline, and *at night let us get up, to give him praise.*

17

HOW MANY PSALMS ARE TO BE SAID AT THESE HOURS?

20 FEBRUARY | [1]We have already mapped out the order
21 JUNE | of psalmody for Nocturns and Morning
21 OCTOBER | Prayer; let us now look at the remaining
Hours. [2]At the first Hour, say three psalms separately,
and not under one *Glory be*, [3]the hymn of the same
Hour after the verse *Deus in adiutorium*, before the
psalms are begun. [4]After the completion of the three
psalms, one reading is to be recited, a versicle, *Kyrie
eleison* and dismissal. [5]The prayer of the third, sixth
and ninth Hours is to be celebrated also in this same
order, i.e. verse, hymns of the same Hours, group of
three psalms, reading, versicle, *Kyrie eleison* and dismissal. [6]If the community be more numerous, the
psalmody is done with antiphons, if, however, small-
er, straight through. [7]The evening assembly however
is limited to four psalms with antiphons. [8]After these
psalms a reading shall be recited, then the responsory,
Ambrosian hymn, versicle, the canticle from the
Gospel book, litany, and the Lord's Prayer before the
dismissal. [9]Compline is limited to the saying of three
psalms. These psalms are to be said straight through,

without antiphon. [10]After these, the hymn of the same Hour, one reading, versicle, and the blessing before the dismissal.

18

IN WHAT ORDER THESE PSALMS ARE TO BE SAID

21 FEBRUARY
22 JUNE
22 OCTOBER

[1]To begin, say the verse: *O God, come to my aid, O Lord, make haste to help me; Glory be*, then the hymn of the appropriate Hour. [2]Then at the first Hour, on Sunday, four strophes of Psalm 118 shall be said. [3]At the remaining Hours, i.e. third, sixth, and ninth, a group of three strophes of the above-mentioned Psalm 118 is said. [4]On Monday at the first Hour, say three psalms, i.e. 1, 2, and 6. [5]And so, each day up to Sunday, at the first Hour, say three psalms in numerical order, but with Psalm 9 and Psalm 17 divided in two. [6]And in this way, Sunday Vigils will always begin with the Psalm 20.

22 FEBRUARY
23 JUNE
23 OCTOBER

[7]At the third, sixth and ninth Hours of Monday, the nine strophes which remain of 118 are said in groups of three at these Hours. [8]Psalm 118 therefore being spread

over two days, i.e. Sunday and Monday, [9]then on Tuesday at the third, sixth and ninth Hours, sing groups of three psalms from 119 to 127, i.e. nine psalms. [10]These psalms are to be repeated always at the same Hours in the same way, until Sunday; the arrangement nevertheless of hymns, readings, and versicles being maintained uniform each day. [11]And in this way, we shall always begin on Sunday by 118.

23 FEBRUARY | [12]Evening Prayer shall be sung daily
24 JUNE | with four psalms. [13]Beginning at 109
24 OCTOBER | they go up to 147, [14]except those which are set aside for various Hours, i.e. from 117 to 127, and 133 and 142; [15]all the rest shall be said at Evening Prayer. [16]And because the total is three psalms short, therefore those of the aforesaid number which are longer are to be divided, i.e. 138, 143, 144; [17]but 116, being short, shall be joined to 115. [18]The order of evening psalms therefore being arranged, the rest, i.e. reading, responsory, hymn, versicle, and canticle shall be fulfilled as we have fixed above. [19]For Compline, however, the same psalms are repeated daily, i.e. 4, 90 and 133.

(24 FEBRUARY | [20]Having fixed the order of daytime
LEAP YEAR) | psalmody, all the other psalms which
25 JUNE | remain shall be divided equally in the
25 OCTOBER | Vigils of the seven nights, [21]dividing

39

those among them which are longer, and appointing twelve to each night. [22]We urge above all, that if by chance this distribution of the psalms should displease anyone, let him arrange it otherwise if he judge better, [23]provided that at all costs he take care that every week the integral Psalter of 150 psalms be sung, always taking up from the beginning again at Vigils on the Lord's Day. [24]Monks indeed who, in the course of a week say less than the Psalter and customary canticles show up their vowed service as far too listless. If only we half-hearted ones could get through in a full week, what we read our holy Fathers strenuously fulfilled in a single day!

19

OF DISCIPLINED PSALMODY

24 | 25 FEB.*
26 JUNE
26 OCTOBER

[1]We believe that the divine presence is everywhere and that *the eyes of the Lord are keeping watch over the good and the bad in every place.* [2]Most especially however, let us, without any hesitation, believe this when present at the Divine Office. [3]Let us therefore always remember

---

* SECOND DATE APPLIES DURING LEAP YEARS

what the prophet says: *Serve the Lord in fear.* 4And again: *Sing the psalms with wisdom.* 5And: *In the sight of the angels will I sing a psalm to you.* 6Let us therefore reflect what one should be in the sight of the Godhead and of his angels, and let us so stand at psalmody that mind and voice may be in tune.

20

OF THE REVERENCE OF PRAYER

25 | 26 FEB. 1If, when wishing to make suggestions
27 JUNE to men in power we do not venture to
27 OCTOBER do so, except with humility and defer-
ence, 2how much more ought supplication be made to the Lord, God of all, with all humility and pure devotion! 3And let us realise that we shall be heard not in much speaking, but in purity of heart and in compunction and tears. 4And that is why a prayer should be brief and pure, unless perhaps it be prolonged by an inspiration of divine grace. 5In the assembled community, however, a prayer shall be altogether shortened, and at the signal given by the superior, let all stand up together.

21

OF DEANS OF THE MONASTERY

26 | 27 FEB.
28 JUNE
28 OCTOBER

1If the community be on the large side, let there be chosen from among them brothers of good witness and holy life and let them be appointed deans. 2They shall take care of their deaneries in all matters, according to the commandments of God and the orders of their abbot. 3Let such be chosen as deans, with whom the abbot can safely share his burdens. 4Nor let them be chosen by rank but according to merit of life and wisdom and doctrine. 5As regards these deans, if one of them, swollen by some pride, be found blameable, if he do not wish to amend when corrected once and a second and a third time, let him be deposed 6and someone else who is worthy be substituted in his place. 7And we ordain the same about the prior.

22

HOW MONKS SHALL SLEEP

27 | 28 FEB.

29 JUNE

29 OCTOBER

[1]They shall sleep singly in single beds. [2]They shall receive bed-clothes which are suitable to the monastic way of life and are distributed by their abbot. [3]If possible, let all sleep in one place, but if the large numbers do not allow this, let them sleep by tens or twenties; their seniors shall be with them to take care of them. [4]Let a lamp be lighting in the same cell all the time until morning. [5]They shall sleep clothed, girded with belts or cords so as not to have their knives at their sides while asleep, for fear they might wound a sleeper by a dream [6]and so that the monks always be prepared. And when the signal is given let them get up without delay and hasten to pass one another out to the Work of God, with all seriousness, however, and restraint. [7]The younger brothers shall not have their beds side by side, but interspersed with those of the elders. [8]As they rise for the Work of God let them gently urge one another on because of the excuses of the drowsy.

23

OF EXCOMMUNICATION FOR FAULTS

28 | 29 FEB.
30 JUNE
30 OCTOBER

1If any brother be found to be rebellious, or disobedient, or arrogant, or disputatious, or to be contrary to the holy Rule in some point, and despising the orders of his seniors, 2he should, according to our Lord's command, be secretly admonished once and a second time by his seniors. 3If he do not amend, let him be reproved publicly before all. 4If even thus he do not correct himself, let him undergo excommunication if he understands what a punishment that is. 5If, however, he be impudent, let him be subjected to physical punishment.

24

WHAT THE NORM OF EXCOMMUNICATION SHOULD BE

1 MARCH
1 JULY
31 OCTOBER

1The degree of excommunication or of punishment should match the nature of the fault. 2The nature of faults shall be left to the abbot's judgement. 3If, however, some brother be found out in lighter faults, let him be de-

prived of sharing at table. ⁴This shall be the treatment
for those deprived of sharing at table: he shall not sing
a psalm or antiphon on his own in the oratory, nor
read a lesson, until he has made satisfaction. ⁵He shall
receive his food alone, after the meal of the brothers:
⁶for instance, if the brothers eat at the sixth hour, this
brother shall do so at the ninth; if the brothers eat at
the ninth, he shall do so in the evening, ⁷until by fitting satisfaction he obtains forgiveness.

25

OF MORE SERIOUS FAULTS

2 MARCH | 2 JULY | 1 NOVEMBER ¹That brother, however, who is entangled
in the guilt of a more serious fault, shall
be debarred from table, as well as from
oratory. ²No one of the brothers shall join his company or converse with him. ³He is to be alone at
the work enjoined him, continuing in sadness and
penance, aware of that frightening decision of the
Apostle, who says: ⁴*Such a one is delivered for the
destruction of the flesh that the spirit may be saved for
the day of the Lord.* ⁵He shall take his meal alone,
in the measure and at the time which the Abbot shall
foresee is fitting for him; ⁶neither he nor the food that
is given him is to be blessed by anyone passing by.

26

OF THOSE WHO WITHOUT PERMISSION HAVE DEALINGS WITH THE EXCOMMUNICATED

3 MARCH | ¹Should any brother presume, without
3 JULY | the abbot's permission, to join an ex-
2 NOVEMBER | communicated brother in any way, or
speak to him, or send him a message, ²he shall incur
a similar sanction of excommunication.

27

WHAT THE ABBOT'S CARE FOR THE EXCOMMUNICATED SHOULD BE

4 MARCH | ¹Since *they that are in health need not a*
4 JULY | *physician but they that are ill*, the abbot
3 NOVEMBER | must look after erring brothers with
great concern. ²And so, as a wise physician, he must
use every remedy. He should send in *senpectae*, that
is older, wise brothers ³who may, as it were, secretly
console the vacillating brother and move him to
humility and satisfaction, and *console him, lest he be
swallowed up with overmuch sorrow.* ⁴Rather, as the
Apostle also says: *Let charity be confirmed towards*

46

him and let all pray for him. 5For the abbot must exercise the greatest concern and move fast most tactfully and painstakingly lest he lose any one of the sheep entrusted to him. 6Let him realise that he has undertaken the care of sickly souls not a violent rule of the healthy. 7And let him fear the prophet's threat through which God is saying: *What you saw was fat you took and what was weak you threw aside.* 8And let him copy the example of love of *the Good Shepherd,* who *left the ninety-nine sheep on the hills,* and went away *to seek the one sheep which had strayed.* 9He took so much compassion on its weakness that he saw fit to *place it on his* sacred *shoulders* and so return it to the flock.

28

OF THOSE WHO, THOUGH OFTEN CORRECTED, DO NOT WISH TO AMEND

5 MARCH | 1If any brother be frequently corrected
5 JULY | for whatever fault, if even excommun-
4 NOVEMBER | icated has not amended, let a stiffer rebuke be given him, that is let them proceed against him with the punishment of rods. 2But if even thus he do not amend, or perhaps—which God forbid— carried away with pride even wishes to defend what

he did, then let the abbot act the wise physician: ³if he has applied poultices, the ointments of exhortations, the tonics of the divine Scriptures, if in the last resort the cautery of excommunication and of beatings with the rod, ⁴and if now he sees that all the pains he has taken produce no result, then let him bring on what is greater—his own prayer and that of all—⁵so that the Lord who can do all things may heal the sick brother. ⁶But if he be not cured even in this way, then let the abbot use the amputation knife, as the Apostle says: *Put away the evil one from among yourselves* ⁷and again: *If the unbeliever depart, let him depart,* lest one diseased sheep infect the whole flock.

29

WHETHER BROTHERS WHO LEAVE THE MONASTERY SHOULD BE RECEIVED BACK

6 MARCH | ¹Should a brother who leaves the
6 JULY | monastery through his own fault wish
5 NOVEMBER | to come back, let him first promise a
full amendment of the fault which led him to leave.
²And so let him be received in the last place, so that
in this way his humility can be tested. ³Should he go

off again, let him be received back in this way up to a third time, knowing that after that every avenue of return is closed for him.

30

HOW BOYS UNDER AGE ARE TO BE CORRECTED

7 MARCH | [1]Every age and mind should have its
7 JULY | own standards. [2]And therefore as often
6 NOVEMBER | as children or juniors or those who cannot understand too well how great a punishment excommunication is, [3]such as these, when they commit faults shall have heavier fasts inflicted on them, or be restrained with sharp beatings, so that they may be healed.

31

OF THE MONASTERY'S CELLARER: WHAT TYPE OF PERSON HE SHOULD BE

8 MARCH | [1]There shall be chosen from the com-
8 JULY | munity as the monastery's cellarer a wise
7 NOVEMBER | person, of mature character, sober, not a gross eater, not carried away by pride, not a trouble maker, not scornful, not sluggish, not a spendthrift,

2but God-fearing. He shall be like a father to the whole community. 3He shall look after everything. 4Let him do nothing without a direction from the abbot. 5Let him keep to his orders. 6Let him not grieve the brothers. 7Should any brother perhaps unreasonably demand some things from him, let him not contemptuously sadden him, but with good sense and humility let him refuse the person's wrong request. 8*Let him keep guard over his soul,* always mindful of the Apostle's saying that *he who will have fulfilled his office well will acquire a good position for himself.* 9Let him take care of the sick, the children, the guests and the poor with total commitment, knowing without a doubt that he will be answerable for all of these on the Day of Judgement. 10Let him look on all the utensils of the monastery and on the entire property as if on the consecrated vessels of the altar. 11He shall not let slide any business as if unimportant. 12Let him not put his mind to avarice nor be a spendthrift and a squanderer of the monastery's property, but let him do everything with due measure and in accordance with the abbot's orders.

9 MARCH | 13Above all let him have humility, and
9 JULY | to the person to whom he has nothing
8 NOVEMBER | to give, let him offer a friendly reply,
14as it is written: *A kind word is better than the best*

gift. 15He should have under his care everything which the abbot shall have committed to him; he shall not presume on those areas which the abbot shall have forbidden him. 16He shall offer the brothers the regular allowance without any arrogance or delay, so that they be not scandalized, remembering the divine word about what is in store for the person *that shall scandalize one of the little ones.* 17If the community be larger, let assistants be given him, so that helped by them he himself may, with a quiet mind, carry out the office assigned him. 18Things to be given out and things to be asked for shall be given out and asked for at appropriate times, 19so that in the house of God nobody be disturbed or distressed.

32

OF THE IRON TOOLS AND MATERIALS OF THE MONASTERY

10 MARCH | 1For the monastery's possessions in iron
10 JULY | tools and clothing and articles of what-
9 NOVEMBER | ever kind, let the abbot foresee brothers on whose life and character he can rely. 2Let him assign each separate thing to them, as he judges fit, for safe keeping and collecting. 3The abbot should keep a written list of these, so that while the brothers

succeed one another in the allotted charges, he may
know what he is giving out and what receiving back.
⁴Should anyone treat monastery material in a slovenly
or careless manner, he should be corrected; ⁵if he do
not amend, let him undergo the discipline of the Rule.

33

WHETHER MONKS SHOULD HAVE ANYTHING OF THEIR OWN

11 MARCH | ¹This vice especially is to be cut out
11 JULY | from the monastery by the roots: ²let no
10 NOVEMBER | one presume to give or receive anything
without a directive from the abbot, ³nor to have
anything of his own, absolutely nothing, not a book,
neither writing-tablets nor stylus, but nothing at all,
⁴for in fact they are not to have their bodies or desires
in their own will, ⁵to hope however for all things
necessary from the father of the monastery. Nor may
anything be had which the abbot has not given or
permitted. ⁶And as it is written, let *everything* be
common to all, nor let *anyone call anything his own*
or presume it to be so. ⁷But if anyone be caught
delighting in this most vile vice, let him be warned
once and a second time; ⁸if he do not amend, let him
be subjected to correction.

34

WHETHER ALL SHOULD RECEIVE THE SAME AMOUNT OF NECESSARY THINGS

12 MARCH | [1]As it is written: *Distribution was made*
12 JULY | *to each, according as any one had need.*
11 NOVEMBER | [2]Here we are not saying that there be respect of persons—far from it! [3]Here let him who needs less thank God and not be saddened; [4]for him who needs more, let his infirmity keep him humble, his exceptions not make him proud, [5]and in this way all the members will be at peace. [6]Above all, the evil of murmuring is not to appear for whatever cause, in any word or sign whatever. If he be caught, let him undergo stricter punishment.

35

OF THE WEEKLY KITCHENERS

13 MARCH | [1]Except for sickness, or if a person is
13 JULY | engaged in something of grave im-
12 NOVEMBER | portance, the brothers shall serve one another so that none shall be excused from duty in the kitchen, [2]because more reward and greater love is thence acquired. [3]Let helpers be provided for the

weak, so that they may not do this work with sadness; 4but let all have helpers in keeping with the
size of the community or the location of the place.
5If the community be larger, the cellarer shall be
excused from the kitchen, or, as we have said, if any
be engaged in more important matters. 6All the rest
shall serve one another in love. 7The server coming
off his week shall wash up on Saturday. 8They shall
wash the towels with which the brothers dry their
hands and feet. 9Both the outgoing and the incoming server shall wash the feet of all. 10He shall hand
in the utensils of his ministry clean and whole to the
cellarer; 11the latter shall hand them out again to the
incoming server, so that he may know what he is
giving and what receiving.

14 MARCH | 12When there is only one meal, those
14 JULY | who are on for the week shall each re-
13 NOVEMBER | ceive some drink and bread over and
above the permitted allowance, 13so that at the
meal-time they may, without murmuring and heavy
work, serve their brothers. 14On solemnities, however, they shall hold out until the dismissal. 15On
Sunday immediately after Lauds, the incoming and
outgoing hebdomadaries should kneel at the feet of
all asking them to pray for them. 16The server coming off his week should say this verse: *Blessed are you,*

Lord God, who helped me and comforted me. 17When
this has been said three times and the outgoing server
has received the blessing, the incoming server shall
follow and say: *O God, come to my aid; O Lord, make
haste to help me.* 18And this, likewise, shall be repeated
by all, and having received the blessing, let him begin.

36

OF THE SICK BROTHERS

15 MARCH | 1Before all things and above all things
15 JULY | care is to be taken of the sick, so that
14 NOVEMBER | service be rendered to them really as to
Christ, 2because he himself said: *I was sick and you
visited me.* 3And: *What you did to one of these, the least,
you did to me.* 4But the sick themselves too should reflect that is for the honour of God that they are being
served, and let them not upset their brothers who
are serving them by their petty, excessive demands.
5However they are to be patiently borne with because
a fuller reward is acquired from such as these. 6There-
fore it shall be the abbot's greatest care that they do
not suffer any neglect. 7A separate cell shall be set
aside for these sick brothers, and an infirmarian
who is God-fearing, diligent and assiduous. 8The
use of baths shall be offered to the sick as often as

is expedient; to the healthy, however, and especially to youths it shall be offered more reluctantly. 9But in addition, the eating of flesh-meat shall be allowed to the very infirm for their recovery; but when they are better again, all shall abstain from flesh-meat in the usual way. 10It shall however be the abbot's greatest care that the sick be not neglected by the cellarers or infirmarians; and he is accountable for whatever fault is committed by the disciples.

37

OF THE OLD MEN AND THE CHILDREN

16 MARCH | 1Although human nature of itself is
16 JULY | drawn to pity for these times of life,
15 NOVEMBER | that is to say of the old men and the children, yet the authority of the Rule shall also look after them. 2Let their debility always be kept in mind, nor shall the rigours of the Rule as regards food be in any way applied to them; 3but let there be a loving care for them and let them forestall the times fixed for meals.

38

OF THE READER FOR THE WEEK

17 MARCH | [1]Reading ought not to be lacking at

17 JULY | the meals of the brothers, nor should

16 NOVEMBER | anyone who takes up a book at random

read there, but a reader for the week shall enter on
his duty on Sunday. [2]After the final prayers of the
Mass and Communion, he who is to begin shall ask
all to pray for him, that God may turn away from
him the spirit of pride. [3]And this verse shall be said
in the oratory three times by all—he however shall
begin it—*Lord, you will open my lips and my mouth
shall declare your praise.* [4]And thus having received
a blessing, he shall enter on the reading. [5]Let there
be deep silence so that no one's muttered criticism,
and no voice except the reader's be heard there.
[6]Whatever is needed for eating and drinking the
brothers shall so pass to one another that nobody
need ask for anything. [7]But if something be needed
let it be requested by some audible sign rather than
by the voice. [8]Nor let anyone there presume to
raise questions about the current reading or about
anything else lest a pretext be furnished; [9]unless
perhaps the superior wish to say something briefly,

for edification. ¹⁰The brother who is reader for the week shall receive a drink of watered wine before he begins to read, on account of the Holy Communion, and lest it be hard for him to endure the fast. ¹¹Afterwards he should eat with the kitcheners of the week and with the servers. ¹²The brothers are not to read or sing each in turn, but only those who edify listeners.

39

OF THE RATION OF FOOD

18 MARCH	¹For the main daily meal, whether at
18 JULY	the sixth or ninth hour, two cooked foods
17 NOVEMBER	are enough, we believe, at every table,

²so that he who could not eat of the one may make a meal of the other. ³Therefore, two cooked foods shall be enough for all the brothers; and should there be fruit or fresh vegetables, let a third be added. ⁴A full pound weight of bread shall be sufficient per day, whether there be one meal or a midday and evening meal. ⁵If they are to eat in the evening, a third part of this pound should be kept back by the cellarer, to be served at this meal. ⁶But should it happen that heavier work has been done, it shall be in the abbot's judgement and power to add a supplement if expedient, ⁷avoiding above all over-eating, so that indigestion

never overtake a monk. 8Nothing indeed is so unsuited to any Christian as over-eating, 9as our Lord says: *Take heed to yourselves lest your hearts be overburdened with self-indulgence.* 10The same amount should not be served to boys under age, but less than to their elders: frugality shall be observed in everything. 11Except for the very weak sick all shall abstain from eating the flesh-meat of four-footed animals.

40

OF THE AMOUNT OF DRINK

19 MARCH | 1*Each one has his own gift from God one*
19 JULY | *in this way and another in that;* 2and
18 NOVEMBER | therefore it is with some misgiving that
we are deciding the amount which others are to eat and drink. 3Nevertheless, looking at the weakness of the infirm, we believe that a *hemina* of wine per day is enough for each. 4But let those to whom God gives the endurance to abstain know that they will each receive his own reward. 5But if the needs of the place or the work or the summer heat demand more it shall lie within the superior's judgement; he shall take care in all circumstances that neither drinking our fill nor drunkenness creep in. 6Although we read that "wine is absolutely not for monks," but because in our times

that cannot be brought home to monks, let us at least agree on this: not to drink our fill, but more temperately, 7because wine *makes apostates even of the wise.* 8But where the needs of the place require it, that even the measure mentioned above cannot be had, but much less, or not even a drop, let those who live there bless God and not complain. 9Above all we admonish them not to complain.

41

AT WHAT HOUR THE BROTHERS SHOULD TAKE MEALS

20 MARCH | 1From holy Easter up to Pentecost the
20 JULY | brothers shall have the meal at the sixth
19 NOVEMBER | hour, and a supper in the evening. 2From Pentecost throughout the whole of the summer, if the monks have not to work in the fields, or if the excessive summer heat does not disturb them, they shall fast on Wednesdays and Fridays until the ninth hour. 3On the remaining days they shall have the meal at the sixth hour. 4This sixth hour for the meal shall be maintained if they have work in the fields or if the summer heat be excessive; and it should be for the abbot to foresee this. 5And let him so time and arrange everything that souls may be saved and that

what the brothers do they may do without justifiable complaint. 6From the thirteenth of September, however, until the beginning of Lent they shall always take their meal at the ninth hour. 7During Lent, however, until Easter they shall eat at Vesper-time. 8The Vespers however should be so celebrated that they do not need lamplight while eating, but let everything be completed while it is still daylight. 9But in every season, the hour whether of supper or of the main meal should be so timed that all be done by daylight.

42

LET NOBODY TALK AFTER COMPLINE

21 MARCH | 1Monks must apply themselves to silence
21 JULY | at all times, above all, however, during
20 NOVEMBER | the hours of the night. 2And therefore in every season, whether of fasting or of midday meal: 3if it be the season of midday meal, as soon as they have risen from supper let them all sit down together, and let one person read the Conferences or the Lives of the Fathers, or indeed something which may edify listeners, 4but not, however, the Heptateuch or Kings, because it will not be useful for weak minds to hear that Scripture at that hour, but let them be read at other hours. 5But if it be a fast-day, when Vespers are

over, after a brief interval let them go on at once to the reading of the Conferences, as we have said. 6And when four or five pages—or as much as time permits—have been read, 7and all have come together during this pause for reading (if by chance someone was engaged in a task assigned him) 8all therefore being gathered together as one body, they shall celebrate Compline, and on going out from Compline no one shall be allowed to say anything further to anybody. 9But if anyone be found to infringe this rule of reserve in speech let him undergo severe punishment, 10unless a need should arise with regard to guests, or perhaps the abbot should order something to someone. 11But even this should be done with all seriousness and the most honourable restraint.

43

OF THOSE WHO ARRIVE LATE AT THE WORK OF GOD OR AT TABLE

22 MARCH | 1At the hour of Divine Office, as soon
22 JULY | as the signal has been heard, dropping
21 NOVEMBER | everything whatever was in hand let
them run at top speed, 2with seriousness, however, so that ribaldry finds no fuel. 3Nothing, therefore,

shall be given precedence over the Work of God.
4But if at night Vigils someone arrives after the
Glory be of Psalm 94—which for this reason we wish
to be said at an absolutely slow pace, with pauses—
let him not stand in his rank in choir, 5but let him
stand last of all or in a place set apart by the abbot
for such negligent persons, so that he may be seen
by him and by all, 6until, at the end of the Work of
God, he does penance by public satisfaction. 7We
have judged therefore that they should stand in the
last place or apart, so that being in the view of all
they may amend for their own very shame. 8For if
they were to remain outside the oratory, there will
perhaps be someone of the type who will go back
to bed and sleep, or at least sit at his ease outside,
passing the time talking nonsense, and an opportunity is given to the Evil One; 9but let them come
in so that they do not lose everything, and let them
amend for the future. 10At the Day Hours, he who
does not arrive at the Work of God after the verse
and the *Glory be* of the first psalm following the
verse—by the ruling we have given above, let them
stand in the last place, 11nor let them presume to
join the choir singing the psalms, before satisfaction,
unless perhaps the abbot, waiving the point, gives
permission, 12in such a way, however, that the one
at fault does satisfaction for this.

23 MARCH | 13At table, however, he who does not
23 JULY | arrive before the verse, so that all may
22 NOVEMBER | say the verse together and pray and all
simultaneously go to the table, 14he who through
carelessness or bad will does not arrive, shall be
corrected for this up to twice. 15lf afterwards he do
not amend, he shall not be permitted to partake of
the common table. 16But let him eat alone, separated from the company of all, his allowance of wine
being withdrawn, until satisfaction and amendment.
17He who is not present at the verse said after the
meal shall suffer a similar fate. 18Nor let anyone take
it on himself before or after the appointed time to
take any food or drink of his own initiative. 19But if
someone refuses to take something offered him by a
superior, he shall receive nothing whatever until fitting emendation at the time when he would like to
have what he refused or something else.

44

HOW THE EXCOMMUNICATED
SHALL MAKE SATISFACTION

24 MARCH | 1Those who on account of serious faults
24 JULY | are excommunicated from oratory and
23 NOVEMBER | table shall lie prostrate outside the

oratory doors saying nothing, at the time when the Work of God is being concluded in the oratory. 2Just placing his head on the ground, he shall lie prostrate at the feet of all as they come out of the oratory. 3And he shall do this for so long a time until the abbot judges satisfaction has been done. 4When he comes at the abbot's bidding, he shall stretch out at the feet of the abbot himself and then at the feet of all that they may pray for him. 5And then, if the abbot orders it, he shall be received into choir or in the place which the abbot has decided, 6with this proviso, however, that he shall not presume to sing or recite alone psalm, lesson or anything else in the oratory, unless again the abbot orders it. 7And at all the Hours, when the Work of God is being completed, he shall cast himself on the ground in the place where he is standing. 8And he shall do satisfaction in this way until the abbot orders him to cease at length from this satisfaction. 9Those, however, who on account of minor faults are excommunicated from the table only shall do satisfaction in the oratory until the abbot gives an order. 10They shall carry this until he gives the blessing and says: 'That's enough.'

45

OF THOSE WHO MAKE MISTAKES IN THE ORATORY

25 MARCH
25 JULY
24 NOVEMBER

[1]Should anyone make a mistake in the recitation of psalm, responsory, antiphon, or reading, unless he be humbled by satisfaction there before all, he shall undergo a greater punishment, [2]as being, in fact, one who was unwilling to correct by humility what he had failed in by negligence. [3]The children, however, shall be flogged for such a fault.

46

OF THOSE WHO ARE AT FAULT IN ANY OTHER MATTERS WHATSOEVER

26 MARCH
26 JULY
25 NOVEMBER

[1-2]Should anyone commit some fault or break or lose something or overstep the mark in any place whatever at any work whatsoever in the kitchen, in the store-room, while in service, in the bakery, in the garden, while working at any craft, [3]and does not come immediately before the abbot and community doing spontaneous

satisfaction, revealing his fault; 4should it become known through someone else, he shall be chastened more severely. 5Should, however, the hidden fault be a sin of the soul, let him make it known only to the abbot (or to the spiritual elders) 6who will know how to cure their own and others' wounds, not uncover and broadcast them.

47

OF TELLING THE TIME FOR THE WORK OF GOD

27 MARCH | 1By day and by night it shall be the
27 JULY | abbot's care to announce the time for
26 NOVEMBER | the Work of God; either by doing it
himself, or by entrusting this charge to such a careful brother that everything may be celebrated at the due time. 2Let those who have been told to do so sing or recite the psalms and antiphons alone, in their rank, after the abbot. 3However, let no one presume to sing or read unless he can fulfil this office so that listeners can build on it. 4It shall be done humbly, gravely, reverently, and by him who is commissioned by the abbot.

48

OF EACH DAY'S MANUAL WORK

28 MARCH
28 JULY
27 NOVEMBER

[1]Idleness is bad for the soul. And therefore the brothers must be employed at certain fixed times in the work of their hands, and again at other times—also fixed—in reading devoted to God. [2]The following plan, we believe, will adjust the time for the one and the other. [3]From Easter until the first of October, going out in the morning, they shall do what needs to be done from the first until about the fourth hour. [4]From about the fourth hour until the time they say Sext shall be reading time. [5]After Sext, however, on rising from table they shall rest on their beds in total silence, or perhaps should anyone wish to read, let him read to himself in such a way as not to disturb another. [6]And let None be anticipated at the middle of the eighth hour, and again let them work until Vespers at what has to be done. [7]Should, however, the needs of the place or poverty oblige them to reap the corn themselves let them not be saddened, [8]because then are they really monks when they live off the work of their hands just like our Fathers and the Apostles. [9]However all shall be done with moderation on account of the faint-hearted.

| 10From the first of October until the beginning of Lent, reading time goes up to the close of the second hour. 11Terce is said at the second hour, and up to None all work at their enjoined tasks. 12At the first signal for the hour of None all shall disengage from their work and be ready when the second signal goes. 13After the meal they shall occupy themselves with their readings or the psalms. 14In the days of Lent, however, let them keep at their reading from morning until the close of the third hour; and until the close of the tenth hour they shall carry out the work enjoined them. 15In these days of Lent let each receive a separate book from the 'library' which they shall read through consecutively from beginning to end; 16these books are to be given out at the beginning of Lent. 17Above all one or two seniors shall most certainly be delegated to do the rounds of the monastery during the reading hours of the brothers, 18and see whether perhaps there be not found a brother who has lost interest, who is indulging in idleness or chatter and not concentrating on the reading, and who is not only useless to himself but is also a distraction to the others. 19If such a one—which God forbid—be found, he shall be corrected once and a second time. 20Should he not change his ways, he shall undergo the correction of the Rule in

such a way that the rest also may have fear. 21Nor shall brother associate with brother at inappropriate times.

30 MARCH | 22On Sunday, also, let all devote them-
30 JULY | selves to reading, except those who are
29 NOVEMBER | deputed to the various duties. 23But if someone be so careless and listless as not to want to or be unable to reflect or read, let him be given some work to do that he be not idle. 24Brothers who are in poor health or who are of delicate constitutions shall be allotted a type of task or craft, that they be neither idle nor overwhelmed by the stress of the work, or run away. 25The abbot must remember their debility.

49

OF THE OBSERVANCE OF LENT

31 MARCH | 1Although the monk's life the whole year
31 JULY | round should be an observance of Lent,
30 NOVEMBER | 2yet because few have this virtue, therefore, we urge one and all to keep their lives in total purity in those days of Lent, 3and in these holy days to atone for what was neglected at other seasons. 4This will be worthily done if we abstain from all vice, if we work at prayer with tears, at reading and compunction of heart, and at abstinence. 5In these

days, therefore, let us increase somewhat our ordinary round of service: prayers on one's own, abstinence from foods and drink, 6so that each one of his own will may offer to God with *the joy of the Holy Spirit* something over and above the norm required of him. 7That is, let him withhold from his body some food, some drink, some sleep, some chat, some ribaldry, and with the joy of spiritual desire wait for holy Easter. 8But this very thing, however, which each is offering, he shall suggest to his abbot and do it with his prayer and goodwill, 9because what is done without the permission of the spiritual father will be lodged to the account of presumption and vainglory, not of reward. 10All things therefore are to be done with the abbot's goodwill.

50

OF THE BROTHERS WHO ARE WORKING FAR FROM THE ORATORY OR WHO ARE TRAVELLING

1 APRIL
1 AUGUST
1 DECEMBER

1The brothers who are working very far off, and cannot arrive at the right time in the oratory 2—and the abbot judges that this is in fact so—3shall celebrate the Work of God at the work site, kneeling down in the fear of

God. [4]Similarly, those who are sent on a journey shall not let the appointed Hours go by, but, as best they can, they shall celebrate them by themselves, and not neglect to offer their daily stint of service.

51

OF THE BROTHERS WHO ARE TRAVELLING NO GREAT DISTANCE

2 APRIL
2 AUGUST
2 DECEMBER

[1]A brother who is sent to do any business whatever and hopes to return to the monastery that same day shall not presume to have a meal while out, even if entreated by anyone whatever to do so, [2]unless perhaps his abbot tells him. [3]Should he do otherwise, let him be excommunicated.

52

OF THE MONASTERY'S PLACE FOR WORSHIP

3 APRIL
3 AUGUST
3 DECEMBER

[1]The place for worship shall be what it is called: nothing else shall be done there, nothing alien to worship stored there. [2]When the Work of God is ended, all shall go

72

out in deep silence, and God shall be held in reverence, 3so that a brother who perhaps may wish to pray on his own may not be hindered by another's impudence. 4But if at other times he wishes to pray more secretly by himself let him, in all simplicity, go in and pray, not with a loud voice but with tears and an attentive heart. 5Therefore, he who is not similarly engaged shall not be allowed to stay on in the place for worship when the Work of God is over— as has been said—lest another suffer hindrance.

53

ON WELCOMING THE GUESTS

4 APRIL | 1All guests who appear shall be
4 AUGUST | welcomed as Christ because he will say:
4 DECEMBER | *I was a guest and you made me welcome.*
2And suitable *honour* shall be *shown to all* especially to *kinsmen in the faith* and to pilgrims. 3As soon, therefore, as a guest is announced let him be met by the superior and the brothers with every loving service. 4And first of all let them pray together and so join one another in a kiss of peace. 5This kiss of peace shall not be offered unless preceded by prayer, because of the devil's disguises. 6In this very greeting, however, let all humility be shown to all guests as

they arrive or depart. 7With head bowed or with the whole body stretched out on the ground, let Christ be worshipped in them: he is being welcomed. 8Once received, the guests shall be led to prayer, and after this let the superior or someone appointed by him sit down with them. 9The Law of God shall be read in the presence of the guest for his edification, and then let all fellow-feeling be shown him. 10For a guest's sake let the superior break his fast, unless perhaps it should be a major fast day which may not be infringed. 11The brothers however shall continue their customary fasts. 12The abbot shall pour water on the guest's hands. 13Both the abbot and the whole community shall wash the feet of all guests. 14The washing completed, let them sing this verse: *We have received, O God, your mercy in the midst of your temple.* 15It is most especially in the reception of the poor and of pilgrims that attentive care is to be shown, because in them Christ is all the more received. Dread is enough of itself to secure honour for the rich.

5 APRIL | 16The kitchen for the abbot and the
5 AUGUST | guests shall be a separate one, so that
5 DECEMBER | guests who turn up at unexpected hours
—and a monastery is never short of them—may not disturb the brothers. 17Two brothers who are capable of carrying out this office well shall take on this

kitchen for a year. [18]These shall be given helpers
when they need them, so that they may serve without
a murmur, and again, when they are less busy let them
go out to work where they are told to. [19]And not
only for them, but in all the offices of the monastery
let this be taken into consideration: [20]that when they
need helpers, they are given them, and again when
they are free, let them obey orders. [21]Similarly, the
guest accommodation shall be entrusted to a brother
of whose soul the fear of God has taken possession.
[22]Beds in sufficient numbers shall be made up there.
And let God's house be served wisely by the wise.
[23]No one who is not authorized to do so shall associate or speak at all with guests; but should he meet or
see them, let him, as we have said, pass on, after
greeting them most humbly and asking a blessing,
saying that he is not allowed to speak with a guest.

54

WHETHER THE MONK SHOULD RECEIVE LETTERS OR ANY THING

6 APRIL
6 AUGUST
6 DECEMBER

[1]Without a directive from the abbot a
monk may in no way accept or give
letters, religious objects or any kind of
little gift from his parents or from anyone else or from

one another. 2But should something be sent to him,
even by his parents, he shall not presume to accept it
unless it be shown to the abbot beforehand. 3Should
he order it to be accepted, it shall be in the abbot's
power to have it given to whom he decides. 4And let
the brother to whom perhaps it had been sent not
despond, lest an opportunity be given to the devil.
5Should anyone presume otherwise let him undergo
the discipline of the Rule.

55

OF CLOTHES AND FOOTWEAR

7 APRIL | 1Clothes shall be given out to the
7 AUGUST | brothers in keeping with the nature of
7 DECEMBER | the places where they live and the weath-
er; 2because in cold regions more is needed, in warm
regions less. 3It is for the abbot to judge this. 4For
our part however we believe that in average places
a cowl and a tunic are enough for each single monk
5—in winter a cowl that is woolly, in summer one
that is light or not new—6and a scapular for work,
shoes and boots. 7Let the monks not make an issue
of the colour or coarseness of all these garments, but
such as can be found in the province where they live,
or what can be bought more cheaply. 8The abbot,

however, shall see to the cut that the clothes be not too short for the wearers, but the right fit. 9On receiving new ones let them always personally hand in the old, to be stored in the clothes-room for the poor. 10It is enough for the monk to have two tunics and two cowls on account of night wear and washing; 11what is over and above this is superfluous; it must be cut off. 12And footwear and whatever is old they shall hand in when they receive the new. 13Those who are sent on a journey shall receive underwear from the clothes-room; they shall hand it back, washed, on their return. 14Both cowls and tunics shall be somewhat better than what they usually wear; they shall receive them from the clothes-room when setting out, and hand them back on their return.

8 APRIL
8 AUGUST
8 DECEMBER

15To furnish the beds let a straw pallet, a light covering, a heavy covering and a pillow be enough. 16These beds, however, are to be frequently searched by the abbot on account of private property, lest it be discovered. 17And should something be discovered with anyone, which he did not receive from the abbot, let him undergo the severest discipline. 18And in order to cut out this vice of private ownership by the roots, let everything necessary be provided by the abbot:

19that is to say, the tunic, the shoes, the boots, the belt, the knife, the stylus, the needle, the handkerchief, the writing tablets, to take away every excuse of need. 20The abbot himself, however, must always reflect on that sentence of the Acts of the Apostles: *Distribution was made to each according as anyone had need.* 21Therefore, let the abbot similarly keep in mind the weaknesses of those in need, not the evil will of those who are jealous. 22In all his decisions, however, let him ponder on God's judgement.

56

OF THE ABBOT'S TABLE

9 APRIL | 1The abbot's table shall always be with
9 AUGUST | the guests and the pilgrims. 2As often,
9 DECEMBER | however, as there are no guests it shall
be in his power to invite whom he wishes from among the brothers. 3Let one or two seniors, however, always be left with the brothers for the sake of good order.

57

OF THE MONASTERY CRAFTSMEN

¹If there are craftsmen in the monastery they shall, with all humility, exercise these crafts, if the abbot gives permission. ²Should one among them pride himself on his mastery of his craft, because he seems to be doing something for the monastery, ³let such a person be removed from the craft, nor let him undertake it again, unless perhaps he humbles himself and the abbot gives him a new mandate. ⁴If anything produced by the craftsmen is to be sold, let those who handle the transaction not dare to cheat in any way. ⁵-⁶Let them always remember Ananias and Sapphira, lest they, or all who cheat from the goods of the monastery, should suffer in the soul the death that these underwent in the body. ⁷In the prices let not evil of avarice steal its way in, ⁸but let the offer always be a shade lower than what can be made by others, the seculars, ⁹*so that in all things God may be glorified.*

58

OF THE RULING FOR ACCEPTING BROTHERS

11 APRIL
11 AUGUST
11 DECEMBER

[1]No easy entrance shall be offered to a person newly come to the monastic life, [2]but as the Apostle says: *Test the spirits whether they are of God.* [3]Therefore, if the newcomer perseveres knocking, and is seen after four or five days to bear patiently the insults offered him and the difficulty made about entry and to persist in his petition, [4]let entry be granted him and let him be in the room for guests for a few days. [5]After this he shall be in the room where the novices learn to reflect, take their meals, and sleep. [6]And a senior shall be appointed to them who has the gift of winning souls and who shall observe them through and through. [7]And care shall be taken whether he is really seeking God, whether he is careful about the Work of God, about obedience, about reproaches. [8]All the hard and bitter things through which one goes to God shall be told him in advance. [9]If he shall have promised perseverance in his stability, after the lapse of two months this Rule shall be read out to him in full, [10]and he shall be told: 'This is the

law under which you wish to serve; if you can observe it, come in; if you cannot, freely depart.' [11]If he still stands, let him be brought to the novices' room mentioned above and let him be tested again in all patience. [12]And after six months have gone round, let the Rule be read out to him, so that he knows what he is coming in to. [13]And if he still stands, after four months the same Rule shall be re-read to him. [14]And if, after having weighed it up to himself, he promises to keep it all and carry out all the orders he gets, then let him be received into the community, [15]aware that he is bound by the law of the Rule and that from that day on he may not leave the monastery, [16]nor wriggle out his neck from under the yoke of the Rule, which, under such long-drawn out reflection, he had been free either to refuse or to take on.

12 APRIL

12 AUGUST

12 DECEMBER

[17]He who is to be received, however, shall promise in the presence of all in the oratory his stability, the conversion of his ways, and obedience [18]before God and his saints, so that if he should ever do otherwise he shall know that he will be condemned by him whom he is mocking. [19]He shall make a written petition of this promise in the name of the saints whose relics are there and in the name of the abbot present. [20]He

shall write this petition in his own hand—or indeed
if he be illiterate another shall write it at his request
—and the novice shall put his mark on it, and place it
by his own hand on the altar. 21When he has placed
it, the novice himself shall intone this verse: *Receive
me, Lord, according to your word and I shall live; and
do not put my hope to shame.* 22The whole community
repeats this verse three times adding: *Glory be to the
Father.* 23Then the novice brother prostrates himself
at the feet of each one, that they may pray for him;
and now from that day on he is considered one of the
community. 24If he has property, let him either give
it away beforehand to the poor, or by a solemnly
attested donation bestow it on the monastery,
keeping nothing back for himself out of it all, 25for
indeed he knows that from that day on he will not
even have power over his own body. 26Immediately
then he is to be stripped in the oratory of his own
clothes which he is wearing, and he is to be dressed
in the monastery's clothes. 27The clothes of which he
was stripped shall be put for safe keeping in the
clothes-room 28so that—God forbid! —should he
ever consent to the devil's persuasion to leave the
monastery, then let him be thrown out, stripped of
the monastery's clothes. 29That petition of his, however, which the abbot took from off the altar, he shall
not get, but it shall be kept in the monastery.

59

OF SONS OF THE NOBILITY OR OF THE POOR WHO ARE OFFERED

13 APRIL
13 AUGUST
13 DECEMBER

[1]Should anyone of the nobility perhaps offer his son to God in the monastery, if the boy himself be under age his parents shall make the petition which we have spoken of above. [2]They shall wrap the petition and the boy's hand in the altar-cloth with the offering; that is how they shall offer him. [3]With regard to their property, they shall either promise under oath in the present petition that never by themselves nor through a third party, nor in any way whatever will they ever give him anything, or give him the opportunity of having anything. [4]Or indeed if they do not wish to do this and want to offer something as an alms to the monastery for their own reward, [5]let them make a gift to the monastery from what they want to give, reserving to themselves if they so wish, the income. [6]And in this way all will be blocked so that not the faintest hope will remain to the boy by which, God forbid, he could be deceived and perish, a thing we have learned by experience. [7]Those less well-off shall do the same. But those who have nothing at all shall simply make the petition, and with the offering they shall offer their son in the presence of witnesses.

60

OF THE PRIESTS WHO PERHAPS MAY WISH TO LIVE IN THE MONASTERY

¹If someone of the order of priests asks to be received in the monastery, consent indeed shall not be granted him too quickly. ²Nevertheless, should he absolutely persist in this application, let him realize he will have to keep the full discipline of the Rule, ³nor will anything be mitigated for him so that what is written will apply: *Friend, for what have you come?* ⁴Let him however be allowed to stand next to the abbot and to bless, and to celebrate Mass, if, however, the abbot orders him. ⁵Otherwise, let him presume nothing, knowing that he is subject to the discipline of the Rule, and let him rather give examples of humility to all. ⁶And should there be question in the monastery of an appointment to office or of some other matter of business, ⁷let him think of his place by his date of entry into the monastery, not of the place conceded to him out of reverence for the priesthood. ⁸Should anyone of the clerics have the same desire to be incorporated in the monastery, let them be placed in a middle rank; and they too, however, if they promise observance of the Rule and their own stability.

61

OF PILGRIM MONKS: HOW THEY ARE TO BE RECEIVED

15 APRIL | [1]Should some pilgrim monk appear
15 AUGUST | from distant parts, and wish to live as
15 DECEMBER | a guest in the monastery [2]and is pleased
with the customs of the place as he finds them, and
does not perhaps upset the monastery by his de-
manding ways, [3]but is simply pleased with what he
finds, let him be received for as long as he wants.
[4]Should he, reasonably and with humble charity,
criticize or draw attention to some matters, let the
abbot prudently reflect whether it was not perhaps
for this that the Lord had sent him. [5]If, moreover,
afterwards he should wish to fix his stability, such a
wish is not to be refused, and especially because his
life could be discerned while he was a guest.

16 APRIL | [6]But if while he was a guest he was
16 AUGUST | found to be exacting or sinful, not only
16 DECEMBER | should he not be incorporated into the
body of the monastery, [7]rather let him be frankly
told to go away, lest others also be infected by his
disease. [8]But if he be not of the type who deserves
to be thrown out, not only if he asks should he be

received to be incorporated into the community, ⁹rather let him be induced to stay, so that others might learn from his example, ¹⁰since too in every place one Lord is served, one King is fought for. ¹¹Moreover, the abbot may place him in a somewhat higher rank, should he judge him to be fit for it. ¹²Not only as regards a monk but also from the above-mentioned grades of priests and clerics, the abbot may establish in a higher place than their place of entry, should he see their life to be such. ¹³Let the abbot, however, take care never to accept a monk from another known monastery as a member of the community without the consent of his abbot or letters of commendation, ¹⁴because it is written: *What you do not want done to you, do it not to another.*

62

OF PRIESTS OF THE MONASTERY

17 APRIL ¹If an abbot petitions that a priest or
17 AUGUST deacon be ordained for him, let him
17 DECEMBER choose from among his own one who may be worthy to perform the priest's office. ²Let the ordained priest, however, be on his guard against vanity or pride, ³nor let him take on anything except what is commanded him by the abbot, knowing that

he must be all the more subjected to the discipline of the Rule. 4Nor let him by reason of the priesthood forget the obedience and discipline of the Rule, but more and more draw closer to God. 5Let him always think of that place which is his by his date of entry into the monastery 6apart from the office of the altar, and if perhaps the choice of the community and the will of the abbot wishes to promote him for merit of life. 7He must know, however, that he has to keep the ruling laid down for deans and priors. 8Should he presume to do otherwise, he shall be judged to be in rebellion, not a priest. 9And if frequently admonished he has not changed, even the bishop shall be called in as witness. 10But if even then there is no amendment, and his faults are glaring, let him be thrown out of the monastery 11should his stubbornness be such that he is unwilling to be subject or to obey the Rule.

63

OF RANK IN COMMUNITY

18 APRIL
18 AUGUST
18 DECEMBER

1They shall keep to their ranks in the monastery as determined by their time of entry into the monastery, their merit of life, and the abbot's decision. 2He, the abbot, shall not disturb the flock committed to him, as if he could arrange anything unjustly by exercising arbitrary power, 3but let him always reflect that he will be rendering an account to God of all his decisions and doings. 4Therefore, it is according to the ranks which he has established or which the brothers have of themselves that they come to the *Pax*, to Communion, to reciting a psalm, to standing in choir. 5And absolutely everywhere age shall neither determine nor prejudice rank, 6since it was as boys that Samuel and David judged the elders. 7Therefore, except for those whom, as we have said, the abbot, for a deeper reason has promoted or degraded for some definite cause, all the rest shall take their place according to their time of entry. 8Thus, for example, a person who came to the monastery at the second hour of the day must know that he is junior to one who came at the first hour, irrespective of age or dignity. 9Children are to be kept under discipline in everything by all.

19 APRIL | 10Let the young honour their elders;
19 AUGUST | let the elders love their juniors. 11In
19 DECEMBER | addressing by name, nobody shall be allowed to call another by mere name 12but the elders are to call the juniors 'brother'; the juniors call the elders '*nonnus*', which is to be understood as

reverence for a father. ¹³The abbot, however, because he is believed to act the part of Christ, shall be called 'Lord' and 'Abbot', not by his own usurpation, but by the honour and love of Christ. ¹⁴Let him, however, think over this and show himself to be such that he is worthy of such honour. ¹⁵Wherever brothers meet one another the junior shall ask a blessing from the senior. ¹⁶When a senior passes by, the junior shall rise and offer him a seat. Nor let the junior presume to sit along with him unless his senior bid him, ¹⁷so that what is written may take place: *Forestalling one another with honour.* ¹⁸Small boys and growing youths shall keep their ranks with discipline in the oratory and at table. ¹⁹Out of doors, or wherever, let them have both supervision and discipline until they reach the age of reason.

64

OF THE APPOINTING OF AN ABBOT

20 APRIL | ¹In the appointing of an abbot let
20 AUGUST | this principle always be kept in mind:
20 DECEMBER | that he be installed whom the whole
community in the fear of God, or even a part of the community—even though small—will have elected by sounder judgement. ²Let him who is to be

appointed be elected for merit of life and wise doctrine, even were he last in rank in the community. 3But even should the whole community—God forbid—unanimously elect a person who connives at their vices 4and these vices somehow come to the knowledge of the bishop to whose diocese the place belongs, or become obvious to the local abbots and Christians, 5let them prevent the consensus of the wicked from having its way. Rather, let them appoint *a worthy steward for the house of God,* 6knowing that they will receive a good reward for this if they do it chastely, with the zeal of God, just as on the contrary a sin if they neglect it.

21 APRIL | 7Once appointed, let the abbot always
21 AUGUST | be thinking of what a burden he has
21 DECEMBER | taken on, and to whom he will be
rendering *the account of his stewardship.* 8And let him realize that he has to help more than to rule. 9Therefore he has to be learned in God's law, to know from where *to draw out things new and old,* to be *chaste, sober, merciful,* 10and let him always *treasure mercy above justice* so that he himself may receive the same. 11Let him hate vices, but love the brothers. 12In the very act of correction let him act prudently and not go too far, lest while he is overanxious to scour the rust, the vessel crack.

13Let him always distrust his own weakness and let him remember *the bruised reed is not to be broken.* 14We do not imply by this that he should allow vices to thicken, but that he should cut them off prudently and lovingly, as he shall see best for each person, as we have already said, 15and let him set himself to be loved rather than feared. 16He should not be restless and a worrier, excessive and stubborn, jealous and over-suspicious, because he will never be in repose. 17Far-seeing and considerate in his very commands, and whether the works he enjoins be of God or of the world, let him be discerning and moderate, 18reflecting on the discretion of holy Jacob who is saying: *If I should cause my flocks to be over-driven, in one day all will die.* 19Taking up these and other examples of discretion, the mother of virtues, let him so attune everything that there be both scope for the strong to want more, and the weak do not turn tail. 20And, most importantly, that he keep this present Rule in all points, 21so that after administering well, he may hear from the Lord what the good servant heard who gave his fellow-servants wheat in due season: 22*Amen I say to you,* he says, *he will place him over all his goods.*

65

OF THE PRIOR OF THE MONASTERY

22 APRIL

22 AUGUST

22 DECEMBER

[1] It happens, rather often indeed, that serious scandals in monasteries arise out of the appointment of a prior. [2] For there are some, bloated by the evil spirit of pride, and looking on themselves as second abbots, take on a tyranny, nurture scandals and make factions in community. [3] This happens especially in those places where the prior is also appointed by the same bishop or by those abbots who appointed the abbot. [4] How absurd this is can be easily understood because matter for pride is furnished him right from the beginning of his appointment; [5] his own thinking suggests to him that he is free from his abbot's ruling power: [6] 'because you also have been appointed by the very same persons as the abbot.' [7] From out of this are stirred up envyings, quarrels, detractions, animosities, dissensions, disorders; [8] with abbot and prior at odds with each other, their own souls, of necessity, run into danger in the course of this dissension, [9] and those under them playing up to party spirit go to ruin. [10] This dangerous evil lies first of all with those who made themselves authors of such a disorder.

23 APRIL | ¹¹Therefore, we see it expedient that
23 AUGUST | the abbot have in his discretion the
23 DECEMBER | running of his monastery, in order to
keep the peace and safeguard love. ¹²And if possible,
let everything useful for the monastery be done by
deans, as the abbot shall arrange (as we laid down
earlier), ¹³so that, shared out among many, no
individual becomes proud. ¹⁴But should the place
require it, and the community reasonably and
humbly ask for it, and the abbot judge it expedient,
¹⁵let the abbot appoint as his prior whomsoever he
chooses with the advice of brothers who fear God.
¹⁶This prior, however, shall carry out respectfully
what the abbot enjoins him, undertaking nothing
against the abbot's will or directive, ¹⁷because the
more he is up in front of others, all the more
carefully should he carry out the precepts of the
Rule. ¹⁸Should this prior be found to have vices or,
taken in by vanity, to become proud, or be proven to
hold the holy Rule in contempt, let him be corrected
verbally up to four times. ¹⁹If he does not amend,
let him undergo the correction of regular discipline.
²⁰Should he not amend even thus, then let him be
sacked from the priorship and another who is
worthy be substituted in his place. ²¹But also if
subsequently he be not quiet and obedient in
community let him even be driven away from the

monastery. ²²Let the abbot, however, reflect that he is giving an account of all his decisions to God, lest perhaps the flame of jealousy or of envy singe his soul.

66

OF THE GATEKEEPERS OF THE MONASTERY

24 APRIL | ¹Let a wise old man be stationed at
24 AUGUST | the gate of the monastery: he will know
24 DECEMBER | how to give and receive a message; his
maturity will prevent his wandering about. ²This
porter must have a cell alongside the gate so that
those who come will always find someone to answer
them. ³And as soon as anyone knocks or a poor man
calls out, let him reply 'Thanks be to God' or 'A
blessing to you', ⁴and immediately let him answer
quickly with fervent love and with all the meekness of
the fear of God. ⁵Should this porter need an assistant
let him get a junior brother. ⁶If possible, however,
the monastery should be so set up that everything
necessary is carried on within the monastery; that
is, the water, the mill, the garden, and the various
crafts ⁷so that there be no necessity for the monks
to be wandering about outside: this is absolutely
not good for their souls. ⁸We wish, moreover, that

this Rule be frequently read out in community, lest any brother make excuses about not knowing it.

67

OF THE BROTHERS SENT OUT ON A JOURNEY

25 APRIL | ¹The brothers being sent on a journey
25 AUGUST | are to recommend themselves to the
25 DECEMBER | prayer of all the brothers and the abbot;
²and a commemoration of all those absent shall always be made at the concluding prayer of the Work of God. ³On the same day on which they return, the brothers who come back from travel, shall lie prostrate on the floor of the oratory at all the canonical hours when the Work of God is being completed; ⁴they shall ask a prayer from all on account of transgressions which may have crept in on the road: seeing or hearing some bad thing, or idle talk. ⁵Nor let anyone dare recount to another whatever he may have seen or heard outside the monastery: it is absolutely ruinous. ⁶Should someone presume to do this, let him undergo the punishment of the Rule. ⁷Similarly, anyone who presumes to go out of the monastery enclosure, or go anywhere, or without the mandate from the abbot to do anything, no matter how small.

68

IF IMPOSSIBLE THINGS ARE ENJOINED ON A BROTHER

26 APRIL
26 AUGUST
26 DECEMBER

¹If some things, perhaps burdensome or impossible, are enjoined on a particular brother, let him, in all meekness and obedience, take on what is commanded by the person in charge. ²But when he sees that the weight of the burden altogether surpasses the capacity of his powers, let him point out to the one in charge of him, with patience and a good moment, the reasons for his impossibility, ³not with pride, nor with resistance nor with contestation. ⁴But if after his statement the superior's command continues the same, let the junior know that this is best for him, ⁵and out of love, trusting in God's help, let him obey.

69

THAT IN THE MONASTERY NO ONE PRESUME TO DEFEND ANOTHER

27 APRIL
27 AUGUST
27 DECEMBER

¹Every precaution must be taken that under no circumstances one monk presume to defend another in the

monastery or to exercise a kind of patronage over him, ²even were they bonded by any degree of blood relationship. ³Nor shall it be presumed by monks in any way whatever, because a most serious circumstance for scandals can originate from this. ⁴But if anyone transgresses in these things let him be corrected more sharply.

70

THAT NO ONE PRESUME TO STRIKE INDISCRIMINATELY

28 APRIL | ¹In the monastery every occasion for
28 AUGUST | presumption shall be avoided, ²and we
28 DECEMBER | lay down that nobody is allowed to
excommunicate or strike any of his brothers, unless it is permitted him by the abbot. ³*Let those who sin*, however, *be rebuked in the presence of all, that the rest also may have fear.* ⁴All shall exercise diligence and supervision of the children up to fifteen years of age; ⁵but this too with all moderation and reason. ⁶He who, without the abbot's mandate, presumes in any degree with an older person, or who flares up without discernment with the children, shall be subjected to the discipline of the Rule, ⁷because it is written: *What you do not want done to you, do it not to another.*

71

THAT THEY BE OBEDIENT
ONE TO THE OTHER

29 APRIL
29 AUGUST
29 DECEMBER

[1] The good thing that obedience is shall be shown by all not only to the abbot, but also let the brothers similarly obey each other mutually, [2] knowing it is by this way of obedience that they will go to God. [3] The abbot's order and that of the persons put in charge by him being dealt with first—nor do we permit private orders to come before this—[4] for the rest let all the juniors obey their elders with all loving solicitude. [5] But if a person be found to be contentious let him be corrected. [6] If any brother, for any tiny reason at all, be corrected in any way by the abbot [7] or by any of his elders, or if he feels that the souls of any elder whatever to be slightly irritated against him, or upset even if a little, [8] immediately without delay let him lie, prostrate on the ground at his feet, doing satisfaction, until this upset is healed by a blessing. [9] Should he despise to do so, either let him be subjected to physical punishment, or if he be rebellious, let him be expelled from the monastery.

72

OF GOOD ZEAL WHICH MONKS MUST HAVE

30 APRIL | ¹Just as there is an evil bitter zeal which
30 AUGUST | separates from God and leads to hell,
30 DECEMBER | ²so there is a good zeal which separates
from vices and leads to God and to everlasting
life. ³Let monks, therefore, exercise this zeal with
burning love, ⁴that is, *let them anticipate one another
with honour.* ⁵And with utmost patience bearing
their weaknesses, whether of bodies or of characters,
⁶let them vie with one another in rendering mutual
obedience. ⁷Let no one seek his own interests but
those of his neighbour. ⁸Let them with purity
offer the love of brotherhood. ⁹Let them fear God
lovingly. ¹⁰Let them cherish their abbot with true
and humble love. ¹¹Let them prefer absolutely
nothing to Christ. ¹²May he bring us all alike to
everlasting life.

73

OF THE FACT THAT THE OBSERVANCE OF THE WHOLE OF RIGHTEOUSNESS IS NOT LAID DOWN IN THIS RULE

| [1]We have composed this Rule, however, so that by its observance in monasteries we could prove that we have at least some decency of behaviour and a first beginning in monastic life. [2]For the rest, for one who hastens to the perfection of monastic life, there are the teachings of the holy Fathers, the observance of which lead a man to the height of perfection. [3]For what page or phrase of divine authority of the Old and New Testament is not the straightest norm for a human life? [4]Or what book of the holy Catholic Fathers does not re-echo how we may reach our Creator in a straight run? [5]And the 'Conferences' of the Fathers and their 'Institutes' and 'Lives', and the Rule too of our holy Father Basil, [6]what else are they but tools of virtues of good-living and obedient monks? [7]But it is double confusion and shame for us, the lazy, the evil-living, the negligent ones. [8]Whoever you are, therefore, who are *hastening to the home country of heaven,*

carry out this very small beginners' Rule, with Christ to help you; ⁹and then, under God's protection, you will arrive at those greater peaks of doctrine and of virtues which we have spoken above. Amen.

Here ends the Rule (for monks).

THE RULE AND THE BIBLE

Notes

CHAPTER 5

5   Ps 18(17):45

6   Lk 10:16

11   Mt 7:14

13   Jn 6:38

15   Lk 10:16

16   2 Cor 9:7

CHAPTER 6

1   Ps 39(38):2-3

4   Prov 10:19

5   Prov 18:21

CHAPTER 7

1   Lk 14:11; 18:14

3   Ps 131(130):1

4   Ps 131(130):2

6   *Cf.* Gen 28:12

14   Ps 7:10

15   Ps 94(93):11

16   Ps 139(138):3

17   Ps 76(75):11

18   Ps 18(17):24

19   Sir 18:30

20   *Cf.* Mt 6:10

21   Prov 16:25

22   Ps 14(13):1

23   Ps 38(37):10

25   Sir 18:30

26   Prov 15:3

27   Ps 14(13):2

30   Ps 50(49):21

32   Jn 6:38

33   non biblical

34   Phil 2:8

36   Mt 10:22

37   Ps 27(26):14

38   Rom 8:36;
      Ps 44(43):22

39   Rom 8:37

40   Ps 66(65):10-11

41   Ps 66(65):12

42   Mt 5:39-41

43   2 Cor 11:26; 1 Cor 4:12

45   Ps 37(36):5

46   Ps 106(105):1;
      118(117):1

47-48 Ps 32(31):5

50   Ps 73(72):22-23

52   Ps 22(21):7

53   Ps 88(87):16

54   Ps 119(118):71, 73

57   Prov 10:19

58   Ps 140(139):12

59   Sir 21:23

61   non biblical

65   Lk 18:13

66   Ps 38(37):7-9

67   1 Jn 4:18

CHAPTER 9

1   Ps 51(50):17

CHAPTER 13

14   Mt 6:12-13

CHAPTER 16

1 & 3   Ps 119(118):164

4   Ps 119(118):62

5   Ps 119(118):164,62

CHAPTER 18

1   Ps 70(69):2

CHAPTER 19

1   Prov 15:3

3   Ps 2:11

4   Ps 47(46):8

5   Ps 138(137):1

CHAPTER 25

4   1 Cor 5:5

CHAPTER 27

1   Mt 9:12

3   2 Cor 2:7

4   2 Cor 2:8

7   Ezek 34:3-4

8   Mt 18:12; *Cf.* Lk 15:4

9   Lk 15:5

CHAPTER 28

6   1 Cor 5:13

7   1 Cor 7:15

CHAPTER 31

8   1 Tim 3:13

14   Sir 18:17

16   Mt 18:6

CHAPTER 33

6   Act 4:32

CHAPTER 34

1   Act 4:35

CHAPTER 35

16   Ps 86(85):17

17   Ps 70(69):2

CHAPTER 36

2   Mt 25:36

3   Mt 25:40

CHAPTER 38

3   Ps 51(50):17

CHAPTER 39

9   Lk 21:34

CHAPTER 40

1   1 Cor 7:7

6   non biblical

7   Sir 19:2

CHAPTER 49

6   1 Thess 1:6

CHAPTER 53

1   Mt 25:35

2   Gal 6:10

14   Ps 48(47):10

CHAPTER 54

4   Eph 4:27; 1 Tim 5:14

CHAPTER 55

20   Act 4:35

CHAPTER 57

5   *Cf*. Act 5:1-11

9   1 Pet 4:11

CHAPTER 58

2   1 Jn 4:1

21   Ps 119(118):116

CHAPTER 60

3   Mt 26:50

CHAPTER 61

14   Tob 4:15; Mt 7:12

CHAPTER 63

6   *Cf*. 1 Sam 3; Dan 13

17   Rom 12:10

CHAPTER 64

5   1 Tim 3:4

7   Lk 16:2

9   Mt 13:52

10   Jas 2:13

13   Isa 42:3

18   Gen 33:13

22   Mt 24:47

CHAPTER 70

3   1 Tim 5:20

7   Tob 4:15; Mt 7:12

CHAPTER 72

4   Rom 12:10